COTSWOLDS TRAVEL GUIDE

2024 EDITION

55+ Cool And Fun Things To Do In And Around Cotswolds

"Embark on an Unforgettable Journey in the Cotswolds"

ROXANNE AZURE

All rights reserved. No part of this book may be reproduced, stored in a retrieval system, or transmitted in any form or by any means, electronic, mechanical, photocopying, recording, or otherwise, without the prior written permission of the copyright owner. The information contained in this book is for general information purposes only. The author and publisher make no representations or warranties of any kind, express or implied, about the completeness, accuracy, reliability, suitability or availability with respect to the book or the information, products, services, or related graphics contained in the book for any purpose. Any reliance you place on such information is therefore strictly at your own risk

Copyright © 2024 by Roxanne Azure

TABLE OF CONTENTS

INTRODUCTION	9
Brief Overview of Cotswolds	9
EXPLORE CHARMING VILLAGES	11
Stroll through Bourton-on-the-Water	11
Discover Bibury's Iconic Arlington Row	13
Wander the Streets of Castle Combe	15
EMBRACE NATURE	19
Hike the Cotswold Way	19
Picnic in Hidcote Manor Gardens	21
Wildlife Watching in Westonbirt Arboretum	23
HISTORIC LANDMARKS	27
Tour Sudeley Castle	27
Discover the Rollright Stones	30
Explore the Ruins of Hailes Abbey	33
HIDDEN GEMS	37
Secret Gardens Off the Beaten Path	37
Local Artisan Workshops in Tetbury	41

| Lesser-Known Historical Sites | 46 |

CULTURAL EXPERIENCES — 53

Visit Shakespeare's Birthplace in Stratford-upon-Avon	53
Explore Gloucester Cathedral	55
Attend a Local Arts Festival	58

CULINARY ADVENTURES — 61

Indulge in Traditional Afternoon Tea	61
Taste Local Ciders and Cheeses	63
Experience a Cotswold Food Tour	65
Cooking Class with Local Ingredients	68
Wine Tasting in Cotswold Vineyards	71
Attend a Traditional Cotswold Feast	75

FESTIVALS AND EVENTS — 79

Attend the Cheltenham Literature Festival	79
Join the Cotswold Lavender Harvest	82
Celebrate the Painswick Rococo Garden Snowdrop Week	85

OUTDOOR ADVENTURES — 89

| Hot Air Balloon Ride over the Countryside | 89 |
| Horseback Riding in the Cotswold Hills | 91 |

Kayaking on the River Thames	94
CYCLING EXPLORATION	**99**
Bike the Cotswold Cycle Route	99
Mountain Biking in Cranham Woods	102
Guided Cycling Tour through Quaint Villages	106
WINTER WONDERLAND	**111**
Christmas Market Magic in Bath	111
Ice Skating in Gloucester Quays	114
Festive Lights Tour in the Cotswold Villages	117
FAMILY-FRIENDLY FUN	**123**
Cotswold Farm Park Adventure	123
Treasure Hunt in Painswick Rococo Garden	127
Explore the Cotswold Motoring Museum	130
SHOPPING AND MARKETS	**135**
Browse the Cotswold Farmers' Markets	135
Antique Hunting in Stow-on-the-Wold	138
Shop for Local Crafts in Chipping Campden	141
LEARN TRADITIONAL CRAFTS	**145**

Cotswold Dry Stone Walling Workshop	145
Willow Weaving in Stroud	148
Pottery Class in Chipping Campden	152

ADMIRE STAINED GLASS — 157

Gloucester Cathedral Stained Glass Tour	157
St. Edward's Church Stained Glass Exhibition	161
Create Your Stained Glass Art Workshop	165

LITERARY HERITAGE — 171

Jane Austen Trail in Chawton	171
Roam the Inspirational Settings of C.S. Lewis	175
Writing Retreat in the Cotswold Countryside	179

GHOST TOURS AND HAUNTED HISTORY — 185

Spooky Evening Tour of Woodchester Mansion	185
Haunted Pub Crawl in Stow-on-the-Wold	189
Cotswold Ghost Stories by Candlelight	192

RELAXATION AND WELLNESS — 197

Spa Day in a Cotswold Retreat	197
Yoga Retreat in the Countryside	200
Thermal Bath Experience in Bath (near Cotswolds)	203

CAPTURE SCENIC VIEWS — 207

Climb Broadway Tower for Panoramic Vistas — 207
Balloon Photography Excursion — 210
Sunset Watching at Cleeve Hill — 213

PRACTICAL TIPS — 217

Transportation Guide — 217
Accommodation Recommendations — 220
Local Etiquette and Customs — 223

TRAVEL ITINERARY SUGGESTIONS — 227

Solo Traveler — 227
Romantic Getaways — 232
Family Friendly — 238
Adventure Enthusiast — 243
Arts And Culture Exploration — 249
Culinary Exploration — 254
GRAND TOUR — 260

CONCLUSION AND REFLECTIONS — 267

IMPORTANT NOTE:

THIS TRAVEL GUIDE IS PRESENTED WITHOUT IMAGES, BUT IT HAS BEEN METICULOUSLY CRAFTED TO ENHANCE YOUR TOURING EXPERIENCE.

Designed as a companion, this travel guide, "55+ Cool and Fun Things to Do in and Around Cotswolds," is intended to provide readers with a diverse range of activities and attractions to enhance their travel experiences. The information contained herein is based on extensive research and the author's personal insights. However, it is important to note that travel conditions, local regulations, and the availability of attractions may change over time.

The author, as an experienced travel guide writer, has made every effort to ensure the accuracy and relevance of the content. Nevertheless, individual preferences, cultural differences, and unforeseen circumstances may affect the enjoyment of suggested activities. Readers are encouraged to exercise discretion and consider their own preferences, limitations, and safety precautions when engaging in any recommended activities.

The author cannot be held responsible for any changes in local conditions, inaccuracies in information, or any incidents that may occur during the implementation of suggested activities. Travelers are advised to verify the current status of attractions, events, and local guidelines before making any plans.

Travelers are also reminded to respect local laws and customs, exercise caution in unfamiliar environments, and make informed decisions regarding their safety and well-being. The opinions expressed in this guide are those of the author and do not necessarily reflect the views of the publisher.

Ultimately, this guide serves as a source of inspiration and information, but readers are responsible for their own travel choices and experiences. Happy travels!

INTRODUCTION

BRIEF OVERVIEW OF COTSWOLDS

Nestled in the heart of England, the Cotswolds is a quintessential region renowned for its picturesque landscapes, charming villages, and rich cultural heritage. This introduction serves as a gateway to the enchanting world of Cotswolds, providing readers with a glimpse into the essence of this idyllic destination.

Geographical Splendor

The Cotswolds, designated as an Area of Outstanding Natural Beauty, unfolds across rolling hills, meandering rivers, and lush valleys. Its scenic beauty, characterized by golden-hued limestone villages, creates a mesmerizing tapestry that captivates visitors from around the globe.

Timeless Villages

Dotted throughout the Cotswolds are timeless villages, each with its own unique charm. From the honey-colored cottages of Bibury to the historic market town of Stow-on-the-Wold, these villages offer a step back in time, preserving the Cotswold's architectural heritage.

Cultural Richness

Steeped in history, the Cotswolds boasts a cultural tapestry woven with tales of yesteryears. From medieval market towns to the remnants of ancient Roman settlements, the region's historical significance is palpable, inviting exploration and discovery.

Outdoor Oasis

For nature enthusiasts, the Cotswolds presents a vast outdoor playground. Visitors can traverse the Cotswold Way, a long-distance footpath offering breathtaking views, or explore the enchanting flora and fauna of renowned gardens like Hidcote Manor Gardens.

Culinary Delights

Beyond its scenic splendor, the Cotswolds beckons with a gastronomic adventure. Local delicacies, traditional pubs, and farm-to-table experiences contribute to a culinary journey that satisfies the senses and immerses travelers in the region's rich food culture.

Arts and Festivals

The Cotswolds is not only a feast for the eyes but also a celebration of arts and culture. Festivals, literary events, and artistic endeavors bring vibrancy to the region, allowing visitors to engage with the creative spirit that thrives in the heart of England.

Embark on a journey through these pages as we delve into the 55+ cool and fun things that await in the Cotswolds, an enchanting destination that seamlessly blends timeless charm with modern delights.

EXPLORE CHARMING VILLAGES

STROLL THROUGH BOURTON-ON-THE-WATER

Bourton-on-the-Water, often referred to as the "Venice of the Cotswolds," captivates visitors with its idyllic charm. As you embark on a leisurely stroll through this enchanting village, the meandering River Windrush will guide your path, flanked by quaint stone bridges that evoke a timeless ambiance.

Riverside Tranquility:

Begin your exploration by the riverbanks, where the soothing sounds of the flowing water provide a serene backdrop. The low, arched bridges add a picturesque quality, inviting you to pause and absorb the tranquil atmosphere.

Bourton's Architecture:

Admire the distinctive honey-colored limestone buildings that line the streets, each with its own unique character. The architecture reflects the Cotswold style, featuring mullioned windows, steep gables, and charming thatched roofs.

Bourton Model Village:

Immerse yourself in a village within a village by visiting the Bourton Model Village. This 1/9th scale replica showcases Bourton-on-the-Water's landmarks and cottages, offering a fascinating perspective on the village's history.

Boutique Shops and Tearooms:

Explore the inviting boutiques and antique shops that dot the village, where you can discover handmade crafts, local souvenirs, and vintage treasures. Don't miss the opportunity to indulge in a traditional cream tea at one of the charming tearooms.

The Motor Museum:

For automotive enthusiasts, a visit to the Cotswold Motoring Museum is a must. Home to a remarkable collection of vintage cars and memorabilia, this attraction provides a nostalgic journey through the history of motoring.

Floral Beauty:

Depending on the season, vibrant blooms adorn the streets and gardens, enhancing the visual appeal of Bourton-on-the-Water. From hanging baskets to well-maintained flowerbeds, the village becomes a kaleidoscope of colors.

Bourton-on-the-Water's Bridges:

Cross the charming stone bridges that span the River Windrush, offering delightful vantage points to capture postcard-worthy views of the village. These bridges are not just crossings; they are iconic landmarks contributing to the village's allure.

Strolling through Bourton-on-the-Water is not merely a physical journey but a sensory experience that immerses you in the timeless beauty of the Cotswolds. Each step reveals the village's rich heritage and invites you to savor the blend of natural splendor and architectural elegance that defines this Cotswold gem.

DISCOVER BIBURY'S ICONIC ARLINGTON ROW

Nestled in the heart of the Cotswolds, the village of Bibury unveils a scene of extraordinary beauty, and at its core lies the timeless charm of Arlington Row. This iconic row of ancient cottages, dating back to the 17th century, stands as a testament to architectural elegance and rural simplicity.

Historical Significance:

Begin your journey by immersing yourself in the rich history of Arlington Row. Originally built as a wool store in 1380, these weavers' cottages were later converted into picturesque dwellings by the influential clothier John Cox in the 17th century.

Cotswold Stone Architecture:

Marvel at the quintessential Cotswold stone architecture that characterizes Arlington Row. The warm, honey-colored hues of the limestone create a harmonious blend with the surrounding landscape, especially during the soft glow of early morning or evening light.

Picturesque Setting:

As you approach Arlington Row, the cottages are reflected in the clear waters of the River Coln, creating a picture-perfect scene that has been immortalized in countless photographs and paintings. The village green, adorned with seasonal blooms, enhances the overall visual appeal.

Photographic Opportunities:

Capture the intricate details of the stone roofs, dormer windows, and climbing roses that adorn the cottages. The timeless beauty of

Arlington Row provides a backdrop for photography enthusiasts seeking to encapsulate the essence of rural England.

National Trust's Recognition:

Appreciate the significance of Arlington Row being recognized by the National Trust for Historic Preservation. This acknowledgment underscores the cultural importance of these cottages, preserving their architectural heritage for future generations.

St. Mary's Church:

Explore the nearby St. Mary's Church, a medieval gem featuring impressive stained glass windows and a peaceful churchyard. The church adds a spiritual and historical dimension to the enchanting atmosphere of Bibury.

Local Craft Shops:

Wander through the village's charming craft shops, where you can find handmade souvenirs and locally crafted goods. This allows you to take a piece of Bibury's charm with you as a memento of your visit.

Seasonal Changes:

Experience the village's ever-changing beauty throughout the seasons. Whether it's the blossoming flowers in spring, the vibrant greenery in summer, or the cozy charm of autumn, Arlington Row adapts to nature's rhythm.

Visiting Bibury's Arlington Row transcends the ordinary; it's an immersive encounter with a living piece of history. As you explore this timeless row of cottages, you become part of a narrative that weaves together architecture, nature, and the enduring spirit of the Cotswolds.

WANDER THE STREETS OF CASTLE COMBE

Castle Combe, often hailed as one of England's prettiest villages, invites you to step into a storybook setting as you meander through its narrow, winding streets. This enchanting village in the Cotswolds unfolds a tapestry of medieval charm and timeless allure.

Cobbled Streets:

Begin your exploration by stepping onto the cobbled streets of Castle Combe. The tactile sensation of the ancient stones underfoot transports you back in time, creating an immediate connection with the village's historical roots.

Quaint Cottages:

Admire the quintessential English cottages that line the streets, each adorned with creeping ivy, colorful flower boxes, and charming doorways. The architecture seamlessly blends medieval and Tudor elements, creating a picturesque scene at every turn.

Market Cross:

Discover the heart of Castle Combe at the Market Cross, a 14th-century structure that served as a market and meeting point for centuries. This iconic landmark adds a touch of grandeur to the village square, surrounded by timber-framed buildings.

St. Andrew's Church:

Immerse yourself in the tranquility of St. Andrew's Church, a medieval masterpiece boasting intricate stained glass windows and a serene churchyard. The church stands as a testament to the village's enduring spiritual heritage.

Castle Combe Circuit:

For motorsports enthusiasts, a visit to Castle Combe Circuit adds a dynamic dimension to the village experience. This racing circuit, set against the backdrop of rolling hills, hosts events that echo with the roar of engines and the excitement of competition.

Bybrook River:

Follow the gentle flow of the Bybrook River as it winds through the village. Stone bridges and charming water features add to the village's idyllic atmosphere, providing serene spots for contemplation.

Old Rectory:

Admire the Old Rectory, a historic building with a thatched roof, surrounded by lush gardens. This architectural gem contributes to the overall pastoral beauty of Castle Combe.

Village Green:

Relax on the village green, a verdant expanse framed by ancient stone walls. This open space invites visitors to linger, enjoy a picnic, or simply soak in the ambiance of this timeless setting.

The Castle Inn:

Unwind at The Castle Inn, a cozy pub with a thatched roof, offering a quintessential English pub experience. Whether for a traditional meal or a refreshing drink, the inn provides a warm and welcoming respite.

Wandering the streets of Castle Combe is a sensory journey through centuries of history, architectural splendor, and natural beauty. The village's timeless allure invites you to slow down, appreciate the details, and savor the magic of a place where the past and present seamlessly coexist.

EMBRACE NATURE

HIKE THE COTSWOLD WAY

Embarking on the Cotswold Way hike is a journey through undulating landscapes and quintessential English countryside, offering a profound connection with nature. This long-distance trail stretches for 102 miles, leading hikers through picturesque villages, ancient woodlands, and panoramic vistas, creating an immersive experience in the heart of the Cotswolds.

Trailhead Excitement:

Begin your Cotswold Way adventure at the trailhead, where anticipation builds as you take your first steps along this historic path. The well-marked trail promises an exploration of diverse terrains, each unveiling a unique facet of the region.

Winding Through Villages:

The trail meanders through charming villages like Chipping Campden, Painswick, and Bath, allowing hikers to absorb the local culture, architecture, and hospitality. The juxtaposition of rural tranquility and village life adds depth to the hiking experience.

Panoramic Ridge Walks:

Ascend to panoramic ridge walks that provide sweeping views of the Cotswold escarpment. Feel the exhilaration of reaching these vantage points, where patchwork fields, rolling hills, and ancient woodlands extend as far as the eye can see.

Ancient Woodlands:

Immerse yourself in the enchanting ambiance of ancient woodlands, where moss-covered trees, dappled sunlight, and the fragrance of wildflowers create a sensory feast. These shaded paths offer a welcome retreat, especially during warm summer days.

Cleeve Hill's Summit:

Conquer the summit of Cleeve Hill, the highest point along the Cotswold Way. As you stand atop this natural vantage point, the panoramic views encompassing Cheltenham, the Severn Vale, and beyond unfold before you, creating a moment of awe.

Historical Landmarks:

Encounter historical landmarks along the way, such as the medieval Hailes Abbey and the grandeur of Sudeley Castle. These sites add a cultural and historical layer to your hiking experience, inviting reflection on the Cotswolds' rich heritage.

Wildlife Encounters:

Delight in the diverse wildlife that inhabits the Cotswolds. From the cheerful songs of skylarks to the sighting of butterflies and rabbits, the trail is a haven for nature enthusiasts, offering glimpses of the region's natural biodiversity.

Charming Pit Stops:

Take respite in charming village pubs and tearooms along the route. These welcoming establishments provide not only nourishment but also a chance to interact with locals and fellow hikers, sharing stories and experiences.

Sunset Serenity:

Experience the serenity of a Cotswold Way sunset. Choose a vantage point overlooking the valleys, and witness the soft hues of the setting sun casting a warm glow over the landscape—a fitting end to a day of exploration.

Accommodations with Character:

Rest in accommodations with character, ranging from cozy bed and breakfasts to historic inns. These overnight stays contribute to the overall immersion into the Cotswold Way experience, offering comfort and a sense of local hospitality.

Hiking the Cotswold Way is not merely a physical journey; it's a holistic exploration that engages the senses, nourishes the spirit, and fosters a deep connection with the natural beauty of the Cotswolds. Each step on this iconic trail reveals a new facet of the region's charm, making it a memorable adventure for nature lovers and hiking enthusiasts alike.

PICNIC IN HIDCOTE MANOR GARDENS

Hidcote Manor Gardens, a masterpiece of design nestled in the heart of the Cotswolds, invites you to indulge in a sensory feast amidst its enchanting landscapes. Picnicking in these meticulously crafted gardens becomes an immersive experience, blending the artistry of horticulture with the simple pleasure of al fresco dining.

Entrance into Paradise:

As you step into Hidcote Manor Gardens, the air is infused with the delicate scents of blooming flowers, creating an immediate sense of tranquility. The meticulously landscaped pathways beckon you deeper into this botanical haven.

Hidden Rooms and Outdoor Rooms:

Explore the concept of "outdoor rooms" as you meander through the garden's unique design. Each area, referred to as a "room," boasts distinct themes, from vibrant flower borders to serene water features, providing a diverse backdrop for your picnic.

The Old Garden:

Choose the Old Garden, one of Hidcote's iconic outdoor rooms, for your picnic spot. Surrounded by yew hedges and featuring a central circular pool, this intimate space exudes a sense of classic charm, offering a peaceful setting for your outdoor meal.

Blooms in Abundance:

Admire the blooms that surround you in every direction. From the vibrant colors of perennial borders to the fragrant roses climbing the walls, the gardens showcase a harmonious blend of textures and hues, creating a feast for the eyes.

Lawn Views:

Spread out your picnic blanket on the perfectly manicured lawns, offering expansive views of the surrounding greenery. The carefully tended grass provides a soft and inviting setting for your outdoor dining experience.

The Pillar Garden:

For a more secluded picnic, venture into the Pillar Garden. This intimate space, framed by stone pillars and adorned with climbing plants, offers a sense of seclusion, allowing you to savor your picnic in a private alcove of nature.

Soothing Sounds of Water:

Find a spot near one of the water features, such as the Lily Pool or the Bathing Pool. The gentle sounds of trickling water create a soothing ambiance, enhancing the overall sensory experience of your picnic.

Architectural Delights:

Marvel at the architectural elements scattered throughout the gardens, including the unique plant structures and sculptures. These man-made accents add a touch of artistry to the natural landscape, creating points of interest as you explore.

Birdsong Accompaniment:

Be serenaded by the melodious tunes of birds that inhabit the gardens. The avian symphony provides a delightful soundtrack to your picnic, creating a harmonious blend of nature's sounds.

Timeless Elegance:

Experience the timeless elegance of Hidcote Manor Gardens as you dine amidst its meticulously curated beauty. The combination of architectural sophistication, floral abundance, and serene surroundings transforms your picnic into a moment of refined indulgence.

Picnicking in Hidcote Manor Gardens is not just a meal; it's a sensory celebration of nature's beauty and human creativity. Each bite is accompanied by the fragrance of flowers, the rustle of leaves, and the visual poetry of a garden that transcends time—a truly enchanting experience in the heart of the Cotswolds.

WILDLIFE WATCHING IN WESTONBIRT ARBORETUM

Westonbirt Arboretum, a living canvas of diverse tree species, beckons nature enthusiasts to immerse themselves in a sanctuary where flora and fauna harmonize. Engaging in wildlife watching within this expansive arboretum offers a captivating glimpse into the intricate ecosystems thriving beneath the canopies of its majestic trees.

Canopy Walkway Adventure:

Begin your wildlife exploration at the canopy walkway, an elevated vantage point that provides a unique perspective of the arboretum. From this height, observe the intricate interplay between sunlight and foliage, creating an enchanting atmosphere.

Diverse Tree Collection:

Marvel at the vast collection of tree species that populate Westonbirt Arboretum. From towering conifers to vibrant deciduous trees, each area of the arboretum serves as a haven for a variety of bird species and small mammals.

Feathered Residents:

Armed with binoculars, spot the diverse birdlife that calls Westonbirt home. Listen for the melodic calls of songbirds perched on branches, and keep an eye out for woodpeckers, nuthatches, and other feathered residents that inhabit the varied habitats.

Sculpted Landscapes:

Wander through the sculpted landscapes, including the picturesque Silk Wood. The juxtaposition of open glades, shaded woodlands, and meandering streams creates a mosaic of habitats, attracting an array of wildlife, from butterflies to elusive woodland creatures.

Pondside Observations:

Approach the tranquil ponds scattered throughout the arboretum. These water features attract amphibians, dragonflies, and a variety of aquatic insects, providing a serene backdrop for observing the natural rhythms of life.

Seasonal Wonders:

Witness the seasonal transformations that unfold in Westonbirt. Spring brings a burst of blossoms and bird activity, while autumn paints the landscape in a palette of warm hues, providing unique opportunities to observe wildlife in different stages of their life cycles.

Badger Setts and Fox Dens:

Venture off the beaten paths to discover signs of mammalian life. Keep a respectful distance from badger setts and fox dens, observing these nocturnal creatures' habitats without disturbing their natural behaviors.

Butterfly and Bee Gardens:

Explore the specially curated gardens designed to attract butterflies and bees. Vibrant blooms not only add splashes of color to the landscape but also serve as a buffet for pollinators, creating a lively dance of wings and delicate movements.

Wildflower Meadows:

Stroll through wildflower meadows, where a tapestry of native plants attracts an array of insects. The hum of bees and the fluttering of butterflies contribute to the sensory richness of these vibrant habitats.

Nature Hide Exploration:

Utilize the nature hides strategically placed throughout the arboretum. These concealed viewing spots offer a patient observer the opportunity to witness wildlife behaviors up close without causing disruption.

Wildlife watching in Westonbirt Arboretum is a captivating journey through the interconnected web of life thriving within its botanical tapestry. From the soaring heights of trees to the secretive habitats on the forest floor, every corner of this arboretum reveals a story of nature's resilience and beauty, providing an immersive experience for those who seek to embrace the wild wonders of the Cotswolds.

HISTORIC LANDMARKS

TOUR SUDELEY CASTLE

Embark on a captivating journey through history as you tour Sudeley Castle, a quintessential English castle nestled in the heart of the Cotswolds. This immersive experience takes you through centuries of architectural splendor, royal connections, and beautifully landscaped gardens, offering a glimpse into the lives of those who shaped the castle's rich tapestry.

Castle Arrival:

Approach the castle through lush greenery, with the imposing facade of Sudeley Castle coming into view. The well-preserved exterior, adorned with towers, turrets, and ivy-covered walls, creates a dramatic first impression that transports you to a bygone era.

Visitor Reception:

Enter through the castle's welcoming gates, where friendly staff provide visitor information and guide you through the ticketing process. The anticipation builds as you step into the historic grounds, ready to explore the secrets held within.

Chapel of St. Mary:

Begin your tour at the Chapel of St. Mary, a masterpiece of medieval architecture. Marvel at the intricate stained glass windows, historic tombs, and the serene atmosphere of this sacred space, which has witnessed centuries of religious ceremonies and royal connections.

Katherine Parr's Resting Place:

Discover the resting place of Katherine Parr, the sixth and final wife of Henry VIII, within the chapel's hallowed walls. The poignant memorial commemorates her life and legacy, adding a historical layer to the chapel's significance.

Queens' Garden:

Stroll through the enchanting Queens' Garden, a meticulously manicured haven that blooms with vibrant flowers and aromatic herbs. The garden pays homage to the queens who once walked these grounds, creating a sensory delight as you explore its charming pathways.

Secret Garden:

Uncover the charm of the Secret Garden, a secluded oasis surrounded by ancient walls. The garden's intimate setting, adorned with roses and hidden corners, provides a tranquil retreat within the castle grounds.

State Rooms:

Step into the opulent State Rooms, where lavish interiors showcase centuries of art, furniture, and historical artifacts. Admire the grandeur of the Banqueting Hall, the regal State Bedroom, and the impressive library, each room telling a story of the castle's evolution.

Tudor Knot Garden:

Explore the Tudor Knot Garden, a geometric masterpiece that echoes the Elizabethan era. The symmetrical patterns of the garden's design offer a visual feast and provide insight into the Tudor influence on Sudeley Castle's landscaping.

Cromwell's Tower:

Ascend to Cromwell's Tower, where panoramic views of the surrounding countryside unfold. The tower's strategic position offers a glimpse into the castle's defensive history and provides an excellent vantage point for capturing the beauty of the Cotswolds.

Visitor Exhibitions:

Immerse yourself in visitor exhibitions that delve into the castle's history, from its medieval origins to its role in key historical events. Interactive displays, artifacts, and informative panels provide a comprehensive understanding of Sudeley Castle's significance.

Dungeon and Wine Cellar:

Descend into the castle's dungeon and wine cellar, where atmospheric chambers reveal aspects of medieval life. The cool, stone-walled spaces provide a stark contrast to the opulence above ground, offering a glimpse into the castle's dual nature as both fortress and residence.

Castle Grounds Exploration:

Roam the extensive castle grounds, taking in the scenic beauty of the surrounding landscape. From the Rose Garden to the majestic yew tree avenue, each outdoor space contributes to the castle's allure, creating a harmonious blend of architecture and nature.

Gift Shop and Tearoom:

Conclude your tour with a visit to the gift shop, where you can find unique souvenirs and mementos inspired by Sudeley Castle. If you desire refreshments, the tearoom provides a cozy setting to savor a cup of tea or indulge in a treat, reflecting on the treasures you've uncovered.

Touring Sudeley Castle is a captivating journey through time, art, and nature. Each step unveils a new facet of its storied past, offering a rich and immersive experience that allows you to connect with the castle's historical significance and the beauty of the Cotswold surroundings.

DISCOVER THE ROLLRIGHT STONES

Embark on a mystical journey through time as you discover the Rollright Stones, an ancient and enigmatic collection of megalithic monuments nestled in the heart of the Cotswolds. This extraordinary landmark, comprised of the King's Men stone circle, the Whispering Knights, and the King Stone, invites you to unravel the mysteries and legends that surround these prehistoric stones.

Approaching the Site:

Begin your exploration by approaching the Rollright Stones, a captivating cluster of ancient stones set against the backdrop of the Oxfordshire countryside. The quiet ambiance and the silhouette of the stones on the horizon create an immediate sense of intrigue.

King's Men Stone Circle:

Enter the King's Men stone circle, where a ring of weathered stones stands sentinel in a field of grass. The arrangement of these stones, varying in size and weathering, sparks contemplation about the purpose and symbolism behind their placement.

Circle Alignment:

Observe the alignment of the stones within the circle, noting their orientation in relation to celestial events. The precision with which the ancient builders positioned these stones suggests a connection to astronomical phenomena, adding an element of celestial mystique to the site.

Whispering Knights Chambered Tomb:

Wander towards the Whispering Knights, a Neolithic chambered tomb located nearby. The stones of this burial chamber lean towards each other, creating an evocative scene that has given rise to local folklore and legends about whispering knights plotting in secret.

Folklore and Legends:

Delve into the folklore surrounding the Rollright Stones, including the local belief that the stones are petrified soldiers, cursed by a witch. The legends contribute to the mystique of the site, offering a glimpse into the intersection of history, myth, and imagination.

King Stone:

Stand before the towering King Stone, a solitary monolith that stands apart from the stone circle. Its distinctive shape and size make it a focal point of the Rollright complex. Consider the theories and interpretations surrounding the significance of this lone standing stone.

Panoramic Views:

Take in the panoramic views of the surrounding landscape from vantage points within the Rollright Stones site. The undulating hills and fields provide a picturesque backdrop, enhancing the sense of connection between the ancient stones and the natural environment.

Seasonal Changes:

Appreciate the Rollright Stones in different seasons, observing how the play of light and shadow, the colors of the landscape, and the weathering of the stones contribute to the site's ever-changing character. Each visit offers a unique perspective on this ancient landmark.

Archaeological Insights:

Explore the archaeological insights gained from excavations and studies conducted at the Rollright Stones. Interpretations of the site's history, its ritualistic use, and its cultural significance continue to evolve, contributing to a deeper understanding of the people who erected these stones.

Wildflower Meadows:

Wander through wildflower meadows surrounding the Rollright Stones, adding a touch of natural beauty to the ancient site. The seasonal bloom enhances the sensory experience, creating a harmonious blend of flora and historic stones.

Visitor Interpretation Panels:

Consult the visitor interpretation panels strategically placed around the site. These panels provide informative details about the history, archaeology, and cultural context of the Rollright Stones, offering valuable insights as you navigate the landmark.

Reflection and Contemplation:

Take a moment for reflection and contemplation amidst the ancient stones. Whether sitting quietly or walking the perimeter of the stone circle, allow yourself to connect with the profound sense of timelessness that permeates this prehistoric site.

Discovering the Rollright Stones is not just a visit to an archaeological site; it's an immersion into the mysteries of the past, where the stones themselves whisper tales of ancient rituals, beliefs, and the passage of time. As you explore this enigmatic landmark, you embark on a journey that transcends the boundaries between history, legend, and the enduring presence of these ancient megaliths.

EXPLORE THE RUINS OF HAILES ABBEY

Embark on a journey through time as you explore the evocative ruins of Hailes Abbey, an ancient Cistercian monastery nestled in the picturesque Cotswold landscape. This immersive experience takes you through the remnants of a once-thriving medieval abbey, revealing architectural marvels, religious significance, and the poignant echoes of centuries gone by.

Approaching the Abbey:

Begin your exploration by approaching the ruins of Hailes Abbey, where the skeletal remains of towering walls and arches emerge against the green backdrop. The abbey's setting, surrounded by meadows and nestled in a serene valley, creates an immediate sense of historical ambiance.

Visitor Entrance:

Enter through the visitor entrance, where the story of Hailes Abbey begins to unfold. Engage with informative displays and orientation materials that provide context about the abbey's founding, its history, and the significance it held within the medieval landscape.

Cloister Walks:

Stroll through the remnants of the cloister, the heart of monastic life at Hailes Abbey. Imagine the rhythmic footsteps of monks as they once walked these cloister walks, engaged in prayer, contemplation, and the rituals of daily life within the peaceful enclosure.

Chapter House:

Explore the hauntingly beautiful Chapter House, where important discussions and decisions took place among the abbey's Cistercian monks. Admire the intricate vaulted ceiling and the remnants of medieval carvings that speak to the craftsmanship of the era.

Abbey Church Foundations:

Stand among the foundations of the abbey church, where soaring pillars and pointed arches once defined the sacred space. Visualize the grandeur of the church, which was central to the religious life of the community and served as a place of worship for centuries.

Altar Area:

Witness the remains of the altar area, a focal point for religious ceremonies and rituals. The solemnity of this space invites contemplation about the spiritual devotion that once filled these sacred precincts.

Lavabo and Fountain:

Discover the lavabo, a structure where monks performed ritual handwashing before meals, symbolizing purity. Nearby, encounter the abbey's original fountain, a source of both practical and symbolic importance for the community.

Abbot's House:

Marvel at the ruins of the Abbot's House, a testament to the abbey's hierarchical structure. The size and design of the abbot's residence convey the importance of this figure within the monastic community.

Dormitory Foundations:

Explore the foundations of the dormitory, where monks slept and spent their nights in communal silence. The austere simplicity of this space reflects the Cistercian commitment to a life of humility and asceticism.

Grave Slabs and Memorials:

Encounter medieval grave slabs and memorials scattered throughout the site, each bearing witness to the lives of individuals who played a role in the abbey's history. These remnants provide a tangible link to the people who lived, worked, and worshipped at Hailes Abbey.

Medieval Gardens:

Wander through the remains of medieval gardens that once adorned the abbey grounds. The reconstructed gardens offer insights into the cultivated beauty that complemented the spiritual life of the monks.

Visitor Center and Museum:

Conclude your exploration at the visitor center and museum, where artifacts, exhibits, and interactive displays provide a deeper understanding of Hailes Abbey's historical and cultural context. Engage with multimedia presentations that bring the abbey's story to life.

Surrounding Landscape:

Take a moment to absorb the serene beauty of the surrounding landscape. Whether from a viewpoint within the abbey ruins or from a distance, appreciate the harmonious integration of Hailes Abbey with its natural setting in the Cotswolds.

Exploring the ruins of Hailes Abbey is a journey into the heart of medieval monastic life, where the echoes of prayer, communal living, and devotion resonate through the stone remnants. The abbey's skeletal silhouette against the Cotswold landscape serves as a poignant reminder of the passage of time and the enduring legacy of this once-thriving Cistercian monastery.

HIDDEN GEMS

SECRET GARDENS OFF THE BEATEN PATH

Discover the allure of secluded and enchanting gardens tucked away from the beaten path in various corners of the world. These hidden gems promise a retreat into nature's beauty, offering a sense of tranquility and a touch of mystery. Explore these secret gardens that captivate the imagination and reveal the magic of nature in quiet corners.

The Lost Gardens of Heligan, Cornwall, England:

Venture into the Lost Gardens of Heligan, a captivating estate that was lost to the wilderness for decades and rediscovered in the 1990s. Uncover secret pathways, ancient woodlands, and the iconic Mud Maid sculpture as you wander through this mystical garden, where nature has reclaimed its rightful place.

Ninfa Gardens, Lazio, Italy:

Immerse yourself in the romantic ambiance of Ninfa Gardens, nestled in the Italian countryside. This hidden gem features the ruins of a medieval town intertwined with lush greenery and a meandering river. The juxtaposition of ancient architecture and vibrant flora creates a dreamlike atmosphere, transporting visitors to a bygone era.

Ryoan-ji Stone Garden, Kyoto, Japan:

Experience the serene beauty of the Ryoan-ji Stone Garden in Kyoto, where carefully arranged rocks and raked gravel create a minimalist masterpiece. This Zen garden, tucked away within a

Buddhist temple, invites contemplation and meditation, providing a tranquil escape from the bustling city.

Huntington Library Desert Garden, California, USA:

Unearth the Huntington Library Desert Garden in Southern California, an extraordinary collection of arid plants from around the world. Wander through a landscape reminiscent of a faraway desert oasis, featuring rare succulents, cacti, and sculptural agaves. This hidden gem showcases the beauty and resilience of desert flora.

Kromeriz Flower Gardens, Czech Republic:

Explore the Baroque splendor of Kromeriz Flower Gardens in the Czech Republic, a UNESCO World Heritage site. Wander through intricately designed parterres, discover the hidden allegorical sculptures, and marvel at the artistic symphony of color and form that defines this secret garden.

Butchart Gardens, British Columbia, Canada:

Delight in the Butchart Gardens on Vancouver Island, a world-renowned horticultural paradise. While well-known, hidden corners within the Sunken Garden and Japanese Garden offer secluded retreats. Experience the magic of blooms, water features, and whimsical pathways that reveal the garden's enchanting secrets.

Claude Monet's Garden, Giverny, France:

Step into the world of Impressionist art at Claude Monet's Garden in Giverny. While the water lily pond and Japanese bridge are iconic, lesser-explored areas like the Clos Normand reveal a symphony of colors and textures. This secret garden reflects Monet's artistic vision and connection to nature.

Kubota Garden, Washington, USA:

Discover the hidden gem of Kubota Garden in Seattle, an authentic Japanese garden nestled within an urban landscape. Serpentine pathways lead to vibrant displays of maples, azaleas, and water features, creating a tranquil escape and revealing the meticulous craftsmanship of this Pacific Northwest treasure.

Jardim do Ultramar, Lisbon, Portugal:

Uncover the Jardim do Ultramar, a secret garden within the grounds of the Tropical Botanical Garden in Lisbon. This hidden oasis showcases exotic plants from former Portuguese colonies, creating a lush haven that feels worlds away from the city's vibrant streets.

Alhambra Generalife Gardens, Granada, Spain:

Step into the Alhambra Generalife Gardens in Granada, where intricate Islamic design meets serene green spaces. While the Alhambra is a renowned attraction, the Generalife Gardens offer hidden courtyards, fountains, and fragrant gardens that transport visitors to a realm of Moorish elegance.

Katsura Imperial Villa, Kyoto, Japan:

Experience the refined beauty of Katsura Imperial Villa's secret gardens in Kyoto. This architectural masterpiece is surrounded by meticulously landscaped gardens that reflect the essence of Japanese aesthetic principles. Hidden nooks and carefully curated views invite contemplation and appreciation of nature's harmony.

Abkhazi Garden, British Columbia, Canada:

Encounter the charm of Abkhazi Garden in Victoria, British Columbia, a hidden gem born from love. Created by Prince and Princess Abkhazi, this garden features lush plantings, winding paths, and unique sculptures. The intimate scale and romantic ambiance make it a secluded retreat within the city.

Hidcote Manor Garden, Gloucestershire, England:

Wander through the hidden alcoves and vibrant "outdoor rooms" of Hidcote Manor Garden. Tucked away in the Cotswolds, this Arts and Crafts garden surprises with its diverse plantings, intricate designs, and secret corners that invite exploration and quiet contemplation.

Parco dei Mostri (Monster Park), Bomarzo, Italy:

Unearth the whimsical Parco dei Mostri in Bomarzo, also known as the Monster Park. This surreal garden, created in the 16th century, features eccentric sculptures of mythical creatures and bizarre structures. The mysterious atmosphere and fantastical designs make it a truly unique and hidden wonder.

Bamboo Forest of Arashiyama, Kyoto, Japan:

Get lost in the enchanting Bamboo Forest of Arashiyama in Kyoto, where towering bamboo stalks create a serene and otherworldly atmosphere. Venture beyond the main paths to discover hidden clearings and secluded areas that evoke a sense of tranquility and wonder.

Tresco Abbey Gardens, Isles of Scilly, United Kingdom:

Explore the subtropical paradise of Tresco Abbey Gardens on the Isles of Scilly. This hidden gem showcases an extraordinary collection of plants from around the world, thriving in a sheltered and unique microclimate. Stroll through terraced landscapes, discovering hidden corners that reveal the garden's botanical treasures.

Rousham House and Garden, Oxfordshire, England:

Uncover the timeless charm of Rousham House and Garden, an unspoiled gem in the Oxfordshire countryside. The garden's naturalistic design, meandering paths, and classical features create an intimate and contemplative space. Hidden surprises await around every corner, making it a tranquil haven for those seeking peaceful reflection.

These secret gardens off the beaten path invite you to escape the ordinary and embark on a journey of discovery. Each one, with its unique blend of natural beauty and artistic design, promises an enchanting experience that goes beyond the surface, unveiling the hidden wonders of the botanical world.

LOCAL ARTISAN WORKSHOPS IN TETBURY

Embark on a journey through the charming town of Tetbury, where hidden among its historic streets are local artisan workshops, each a treasure trove of craftsmanship and creativity. These hidden gems offer an immersive experience, allowing visitors to witness the skillful hands and artistic passion behind unique, handmade creations. Explore Tetbury's artisan scene, where tradition meets innovation in the heart of the Cotswolds.

The Tetbury Edit: Bespoke Leather Goods Studio:

Step into The Tetbury Edit, a bespoke leather goods studio where skilled artisans meticulously craft handmade leather products. From artisanal wallets to custom-designed bags, witness the fusion of traditional craftsmanship and contemporary design. Engage with the artisans, and even customize your own piece, creating a one-of-a-kind souvenir.

Cotswold Woolen Weavers:

Immerse yourself in the age-old craft of weaving at Cotswold Woolen Weavers. This hidden gem showcases the artistry of handloom weaving, producing an array of beautifully textured fabrics. Feel the softness of locally sourced wool and witness the rhythmic dance of the looms as intricate patterns come to life, preserving a rich textile tradition.

Tetbury Uplands Pottery Studio:

Uncover the Tetbury Uplands Pottery Studio, where a potter's wheel transforms clay into functional and artistic pieces. Watch as artisans shape and mold the clay, creating unique pottery that reflects the beauty of the Cotswold landscape. The studio's rustic charm and the hands-on experience offer a glimpse into the world of ceramic craftsmanship.

Artisan Chocolate Haven:

Indulge your senses at the Artisan Chocolate Haven, a local chocolatier crafting exquisite handmade chocolates. Delight in the aroma of cocoa as skilled artisans temper, mold, and hand-paint each chocolate creation. Experience a chocolate tasting session and discover the artistry behind creating delectable treats that capture the essence of Tetbury.

Cotswold Stone Masonry Workshop:

Enter the Cotswold Stone Masonry Workshop, where ancient techniques meet contemporary design in the crafting of stone.

Artisans carve and shape local limestone into intricate sculptures and architectural elements. Witness the precision of stone carving and learn about the historical significance of this timeless craft in the Cotswolds.

Bespoke Floral Atelier:

Explore a bespoke floral atelier, where florists transform blooms into artful arrangements. From hand-tied bouquets to intricate floral installations, the atelier showcases the art of floral design. Engage with the artisans as they share their expertise, and perhaps even participate in a floral arranging workshop to take home your own creation.

Tetbury Textile Art Studio:

Immerse yourself in the Tetbury Textile Art Studio, a haven for fabric enthusiasts and textile artists. Admire the vibrant array of fabrics, threads, and creations, and witness textile artisans at work. Participate in a hands-on workshop to learn traditional techniques or experiment with contemporary textile art forms, adding a personal touch to your Tetbury experience.

Traditional Bookbinding Nook:

Step into a traditional bookbinding nook, where skilled craftsmen meticulously bind and restore books by hand. The fragrance of leather and the sight of antique presses evoke a sense of nostalgia. Witness the art of bookbinding unfold as artisans preserve both the written word and the craftsmanship of centuries past.

Tetbury Candle Artisan's Workshop:

Illuminate your senses at the Tetbury Candle Artisan's Workshop, where candles are hand-poured and sculpted into works of art.

Engage with candle artisans as they demonstrate the intricate process of crafting unique, fragrant candles. Discover the art of creating bespoke candles that capture the essence of Tetbury's charm.

The Tetbury Silversmith's Forge:

Step into The Tetbury Silversmith's Forge, a haven for silver enthusiasts and jewelry aficionados. Watch as skilled silversmiths shape precious metals into intricate designs, creating bespoke jewelry pieces. Whether observing the delicate art of filigree or trying your hand at jewelry making, the forge offers an intimate glimpse into the world of fine craftsmanship.

Cotswold Ceramics Collective:

Explore the Cotswold Ceramics Collective, a collaborative space where ceramic artists showcase their individual styles and techniques. From wheel-thrown pottery to hand-built sculptures, witness the diversity of contemporary ceramics. Engage with the artists, attend workshops, and even acquire unique ceramic pieces that reflect the artistic energy of Tetbury.

Bicycle Craftsmanship Haven:

Pedal into a bicycle craftsmanship haven, where artisans handcraft and customize bicycles. Marvel at the meticulous attention to detail as frames are shaped, gears are tuned, and wheels are true. Engage with bicycle craftsmen to create a personalized ride, combining functionality with bespoke design in the heart of Tetbury.

The Tetbury Glassblower's Studio:

Witness the mesmerizing dance of molten glass at The Tetbury Glassblower's Studio. Skilled glass artists shape and sculpt vibrant glass creations, from delicate ornaments to intricate glassware. Take a front-row seat to the glassblowing process, or participate in a workshop to try your hand at crafting your own glass masterpiece.

Artisan Perfumery Workshop:

Engage your olfactory senses at an artisan perfumery workshop, where fragrances are crafted by skilled perfumers. Discover the art of blending essential oils and creating bespoke scents that capture the essence of Tetbury. Participate in a fragrance-making workshop to design a signature scent that becomes a unique memento of your visit.

Woodcraft Artisans Guild:

Enter the Woodcraft Artisans Guild, where skilled woodworkers shape and carve wood into functional and artistic pieces. From handcrafted furniture to intricately carved sculptures, witness the marriage of craftsmanship and natural beauty. Engage with woodcraft artisans, and perhaps take home a bespoke wooden creation as a lasting reminder of Tetbury.

Tetbury Art Gallery and Studio Spaces:

Immerse yourself in Tetbury's vibrant art scene by exploring local art galleries and studio spaces. Discover a diverse range of artistic expressions, from paintings to sculptures, and engage with resident artists. Attend gallery openings, workshops, and art events that showcase the dynamic creativity thriving in Tetbury.

The Tetbury Clockmaker's Workshop:

Step into The Tetbury Clockmaker's Workshop, where timepieces are meticulously crafted and restored by skilled clockmakers.

Experience the delicate art of horology as intricate mechanisms come to life. Engage with the clockmakers to learn about the history of timekeeping and perhaps acquire a timeless piece that echoes Tetbury's enduring charm.

These hidden gems of local artisan workshops in Tetbury beckon you to explore the town's creative soul. From traditional crafts to contemporary expressions, each workshop offers a unique window into the world of craftsmanship and artistic passion that defines Tetbury's cultural tapestry.

LESSER-KNOWN HISTORICAL SITES

Embark on a journey through history, uncovering the lesser-known historical sites that breathe life into the past. These hidden gems, tucked away from the bustling tourist trails, reveal captivating stories, architectural marvels, and a sense of heritage waiting to be explored. From forgotten castles to ancient ruins, each site carries a unique charm that invites the curious traveler to step back in time.

Sudeley Castle's Secret Gardens, Gloucestershire, England:

Venture beyond the well-known halls of Sudeley Castle and discover its hidden gem—the Secret Gardens. Tucked away within the castle grounds, these gardens boast centuries-old yew hedges, vibrant floral displays, and a serene pond. Uncover the romantic charm and historical significance of this lesser-explored corner, where queens walked and intrigue unfolded.

Rollright Stones, Oxfordshire, England:

Explore the enigmatic Rollright Stones, a prehistoric complex shrouded in mystery. Beyond the famous King Stone and Whispering Knights, lesser-known stones are scattered across the landscape. Delve into the folklore and legends surrounding this ancient site, where the stones are said to dance at night, and experience the mystical ambiance that permeates the Rollright Hills.

Hailes Abbey Ruins, Gloucestershire, England:

Wander through the hauntingly beautiful ruins of Hailes Abbey, hidden in the Gloucestershire countryside. Once a Cistercian monastery, the abbey fell into disrepair during the Dissolution. Explore the skeletal remains of the church, cloisters, and chapter house, and imagine the echoes of medieval chants that once filled the air.

Crickley Hill Neolithic Enclosure, Gloucestershire, England:

Step back in time at Crickley Hill, where a Neolithic enclosure stands as a testament to ancient engineering. This lesser-known site features earthworks dating back thousands of years, offering a glimpse into the lives of early settlers. Walk the perimeter of the enclosure and marvel at the panoramic views of the surrounding landscape.

Stanway House and Fountain, Gloucestershire, England:

Discover the hidden splendor of Stanway House, a Jacobean manor with a surprise in its gardens—the tallest gravity fountain in the world. Tucked away in the Cotswold countryside, this lesser-known gem allows visitors to witness the dramatic display as water shoots skyward from the gravity-fed fountain, creating a spectacle amidst the historic estate.

Beverston Castle Ruins, Gloucestershire, England:

Explore the quiet ruins of Beverston Castle, a medieval fortress steeped in history. Nestled in a secluded corner of the Cotswolds, this lesser-known site invites you to wander through the remains of towers and walls that once played a role in the tumultuous events of the past. Experience the serene atmosphere and imagine the castle in its prime.

Notgrove Long Barrow, Gloucestershire, England:

Encounter the ancient mystery of Notgrove Long Barrow, a Neolithic burial mound hidden in the Gloucestershire countryside. This lesser-known archaeological gem offers a glimpse into prehistoric burial practices. Enter the chambered tomb and reflect on the passage of time, surrounded by the quietude of the landscape.

Haughmond Abbey, Shropshire, England:

Uncover the peaceful ruins of Haughmond Abbey, a lesser-explored Cistercian monastery dating back to the 12th century. Tucked away in the Shropshire countryside, the abbey invites contemplation as visitors stroll through the nave, chapter house, and cloister. Experience the serenity of this hidden historical site, where echoes of medieval life linger.

Broughton Castle, Oxfordshire, England:

Venture beyond the well-known landmarks to discover the charm of Broughton Castle. This lesser-explored gem boasts a well-preserved medieval courtyard and picturesque gardens. Wander through the historic rooms filled with tapestries and period furniture, and appreciate the timeless beauty of this hidden castle in the heart of Oxfordshire.

Cricklade, Saxon Wall and Ditches, Wiltshire, England:

Explore the remnants of Cricklade's Saxon Wall and Ditches, a lesser-known archaeological site in Wiltshire. These earthworks, believed to date back to the Saxon period, provide a glimpse into the town's early defenses. Walk along the ancient walls and imagine the history that unfolded within and around this hidden historical site.

Minster Lovell Hall, Oxfordshire, England:

Discover the atmospheric ruins of Minster Lovell Hall, nestled along the River Windrush. This lesser-known medieval manor, abandoned in the 18th century, retains its haunting beauty. Stroll through the remains of the great hall, tower, and gatehouse, and sense the echoes of a bygone era in this hidden corner of Oxfordshire.

Bibury Trout Farm, Gloucestershire, England:

Visit Bibury Trout Farm, not just for its pisciculture but for its historical charm. This lesser-known gem has been operating since the 1900s and offers a glimpse into traditional trout farming practices. Explore the picturesque grounds, stroll along the water, and appreciate the blend of history and nature in this Cotswold gem.

Nympsfield Long Barrow, Gloucestershire, England:

Encounter the ancient mystery of Nympsfield Long Barrow, a Neolithic burial mound overlooking the Severn Valley. This lesser-known archaeological site provides insight into the rituals of ancient communities. Ascend to the barrow's summit for panoramic views and contemplate the enduring legacy of those who once revered this sacred landscape.

Great Tew Circle, Oxfordshire, England:

Step into the past at Great Tew Circle, a lesser-known stone circle hidden in the Oxfordshire countryside. While smaller than its famous counterparts, the circle holds archaeological significance. Wander among the standing stones and ponder the rituals and beliefs of the ancient communities that once gathered in this tranquil setting.

Tolsey Museum, Burford, Oxfordshire, England:

Explore the hidden treasures of Tolsey Museum in Burford, a lesser-known gem that houses a collection of artifacts and exhibits showcasing the town's history. From medieval coins to vintage household items, this museum offers a charming journey through the lesser-known aspects of Burford's past.

King's Stanley Almshouses, Gloucestershire, England:

Discover the historical charm of King's Stanley Almshouses, a lesser-known architectural gem in the Cotswolds. These almshouses, built in the 17th century, reflect the philanthropic efforts of the past. Wander through the courtyard and appreciate the enduring legacy of this hidden historical site.

Kiftsgate Court Gardens, Gloucestershire, England:

Explore the lesser-known beauty of Kiftsgate Court Gardens, a stunning horticultural masterpiece hidden in the Cotswolds. While the gardens are celebrated, their unique charm often escapes the main spotlight. Meander through terraced levels, discover hidden corners, and appreciate the floral artistry that defines this Cotswold gem.

These lesser-known historical sites weave a tapestry of stories, architecture, and traditions that enrich the cultural heritage of the Cotswolds. Venture off the beaten path to uncover these hidden gems, each a portal to a bygone era waiting to be explored and appreciated.

CULTURAL EXPERIENCES

VISIT SHAKESPEARE'S BIRTHPLACE IN STRATFORD-UPON-AVON

Stepping into the hallowed halls of Shakespeare's Birthplace in Stratford-upon-Avon is a pilgrimage into the life and times of the world's greatest playwright. This historic site, meticulously preserved, invites visitors to immerse themselves in the very place where William Shakespeare took his first breath and began his remarkable journey.

Entrance Courtyard:

Your cultural odyssey begins in the entrance courtyard, where the Tudor architecture of the birthplace sets the stage for the immersive experience that awaits. Timber-framed structures and a sense of historical grandeur create an immediate connection to the 16th-century world.

Birth Room:

Ascend the creaking wooden staircase to Shakespeare's birthroom, the very chamber where the literary genius was born in 1564. The room is adorned with period furniture and authentic memorabilia, offering an intimate glimpse into the humble beginnings of a literary giant.

Exhibition Displays:

Explore the exhibition spaces, where interactive displays and artifacts narrate the tale of Shakespeare's life. Manuscripts, personal belongings, and rare documents provide a vivid context for understanding the playwright's cultural and historical significance.

Garden of Remembrance:

Wander through the tranquil Garden of Remembrance, where fragrant herbs and vibrant flowers surround a statue of Shakespeare. This peaceful oasis offers a reflective space to ponder the enduring impact of the Bard's contributions to literature.

Tread the Floorboards:

Step onto the aged floorboards of the birthplace, which have borne witness to centuries of history. The creaking sounds beneath your feet echo the passage of time and the countless admirers who have trodden this literary pilgrimage.

Quill and Ink Demonstrations:

Witness live demonstrations of quill and ink writing, harkening back to the methods Shakespeare himself would have employed. Engage in the tactile experience of using traditional writing tools, connecting with the artistry of the written word.

Costumed Guides:

Encounter costumed guides who embody characters from Shakespeare's plays. Their engaging narratives bring the past to life, offering insights into the daily life, societal norms, and theatrical world of Elizabethan England.

Shakespeare Aloud Performances:

Attend Shakespeare Aloud performances within the birthplace, where talented actors bring excerpts from the Bard's plays to life.

The intimate setting and period-appropriate ambiance enhance the immersive nature of these live interpretations.

Mulberry Tree:

Pause by the ancient Mulberry Tree in the garden, rumored to have been planted by Shakespeare himself. The gnarled branches and vibrant foliage contribute to the mythic quality of the birthplace's surroundings.

Gift Shop:

Conclude your visit with a stop at the gift shop, where you can acquire Shakespearean mementos, literary works, and period-inspired souvenirs. The shop extends the cultural experience, allowing you to take a piece of Shakespeare's legacy home.

Visiting Shakespeare's Birthplace is not just a tour; it's a profound cultural journey that bridges the centuries. It invites you to walk in the footsteps of a literary giant, to touch the relics of history, and to marvel at the enduring legacy of a playwright whose words continue to resonate across the globe.

EXPLORE GLOUCESTER CATHEDRAL

Embarking on a cultural exploration of Gloucester Cathedral is an awe-inspiring journey through centuries of history, architectural marvels, and spiritual significance. This sacred site, with its soaring Gothic architecture, intricately carved details, and rich cultural heritage, beckons visitors to uncover the stories embedded within its hallowed walls.

Exterior Grandeur:

Approach the cathedral from College Green, where the sheer grandeur of its exterior comes into view. The majestic facade, adorned with delicate tracery and towering spires, sets a tone of reverence and anticipation.

West Front Sculptures:

Marvel at the West Front sculptures, a masterpiece of medieval artistry. The intricate carvings depict biblical scenes, saints, and angels, inviting contemplation on the craftsmanship and spiritual narratives woven into the stone.

Cloistered Courtyard:

Enter the cloistered courtyard, an oasis of tranquility surrounded by the cathedral's walls. The cloisters, with their rib-vaulted ceilings and graceful arches, exude a sense of serenity, providing a contemplative space for reflection.

Medieval Chapter House:

Explore the medieval Chapter House, renowned for its stunning fan vaulting. This octagonal space served as a meeting place for the cathedral's clergy, and its architectural splendor reflects the Gothic mastery of the craftsmen who shaped it.

Whispering Gallery:

Ascend to the Whispering Gallery, where the acoustics allow for whispers to be heard across the vast space. This architectural marvel provides a unique vantage point, offering panoramic views of the cathedral interior and a chance to absorb the intricate details of the vaulted ceiling.

Lady Chapel:

Enter the Lady Chapel, an exquisite example of Perpendicular Gothic architecture. The large windows flood the chapel with natural light, illuminating the intricate stonework and creating a serene atmosphere for contemplation and prayer.

Great East Window:

Stand in awe before the Great East Window, a masterpiece of medieval stained glass. The vibrant hues and intricate detailing of biblical narratives make this window a captivating focal point, showcasing the fusion of art and spirituality.

Tombs and Memorials:

Discover the tombs and memorials scattered throughout the cathedral, each telling a story of individuals who played significant roles in the cathedral's history. From bishops to monarchs, these commemorative monuments offer glimpses into the lives of those laid to rest within its sacred precincts.

Cathedral Library:

Visit the Cathedral Library, a hidden gem that houses rare manuscripts, ancient texts, and historical documents. The serene ambiance of the library provides a quiet retreat for delving into the cathedral's rich literary heritage.

Choral Evensong:

If timing permits, attend a Choral Evensong service, where the resonant voices of the cathedral choir fill the sacred space. The spiritual and musical experience adds a profound layer to your cultural exploration, allowing you to partake in the cathedral's living tradition.

Exploring Gloucester Cathedral is a multi-sensory encounter with history, spirituality, and architectural splendor. Each step unveils a new facet of the cathedral's cultural significance, inviting visitors to connect with the past and appreciate the enduring beauty of this sacred sanctuary in the heart of Gloucester.

ATTEND A LOCAL ARTS FESTIVAL

Participating in a local arts festival is an immersive journey into the vibrant tapestry of a community's creativity, diversity, and cultural expression. From visual arts to live performances, culinary delights, and interactive installations, these festivals serve as dynamic showcases of the local arts scene, fostering a sense of community and celebration.

Festival Grounds Atmosphere:

Step onto the festival grounds, where an atmosphere of excitement and creativity permeates the air. Vibrant colors, eclectic decorations, and the hum of anticipation set the stage for a cultural extravaganza that promises to engage the senses.

Visual Arts Exhibitions:

Immerse yourself in visual arts exhibitions that showcase the talent and innovation of local artists. Wander through galleries, open-air displays, and pop-up installations, where paintings, sculptures, and mixed-media creations invite contemplation and dialogue.

Street Performers and Buskers:

Encounter street performers and buskers who bring the streets to life with their talents. From musicians and dancers to living statues and circus acts, these performers contribute to the festive ambiance, creating spontaneous moments of joy and entertainment.

Live Music Stages:

Explore live music stages featuring a diverse lineup of local bands and artists. The sounds of various genres—from folk and jazz to indie and world music—create a melodic backdrop, inviting festivalgoers to discover new musical expressions.

Culinary Delights:

Indulge in culinary delights from local food vendors and artisanal stalls. From international cuisines to gourmet treats, the festival becomes a gastronomic journey where flavors and aromas add to the overall sensory experience.

Interactive Workshops:

Engage in interactive workshops that invite hands-on participation. Whether it's pottery, painting, or dance, these workshops provide an opportunity to connect with local artisans, learn new skills, and unleash your own creative potential.

Literary Events and Readings:

Attend literary events and readings that celebrate local authors and poets. Book tents and author meet-and-greets offer a space for literary enthusiasts to explore the written word and engage in discussions about storytelling and creativity.

Cultural Performances:

Witness cultural performances that showcase traditional dance, music, and theatrical arts. These performances provide a window into the rich cultural heritage of the community, fostering an appreciation for diversity and heritage.

Artisan Markets:

Explore artisan markets featuring handmade crafts, jewelry, and unique creations by local artisans. These markets provide an opportunity to support local businesses and take home one-of-a-kind treasures that encapsulate the festival's spirit.

Community Engagement:

Participate in community engagement activities that foster connections and dialogue. From panel discussions to forums on the intersection of arts and society, these sessions contribute to the festival's role as a platform for cultural exchange and collective reflection.

Attending a local arts festival is not just a cultural outing; it's an immersive celebration of community, creativity, and shared expression. It invites you to explore, interact, and be inspired by the myriad forms of artistic expression that collectively define the identity and vibrancy of a local culture.

CULINARY ADVENTURES

INDULGE IN TRADITIONAL AFTERNOON TEA

Embarking on the ritual of traditional afternoon tea is a delightful journey into elegance, charm, and culinary refinement. Rooted in British tradition, this culinary experience goes beyond a simple meal; it is a celebration of delectable treats, fine teas, and the art of savoring moments of indulgence.

Charming Setting:

Step into a charming tea room or an opulent hotel lounge, where the ambiance is infused with a sense of sophistication. Crystal chandeliers, delicate table settings, and plush seating create an inviting space for an afternoon of indulgence.

Selection of Teas:

Begin your culinary journey by selecting from an extensive array of teas. From classic blends like Earl Grey and English Breakfast to aromatic herbal infusions, each tea is curated to complement the flavors of the accompanying treats.

Elegant Tea Service:

Experience the elegance of a traditional tea service, where a dedicated server attends to your needs. The careful pouring of tea into delicate china cups adds a touch of ceremony to the proceedings, setting the tone for a refined experience.

Savory Sandwiches:

Delight in an assortment of savory sandwiches, meticulously crafted with the finest ingredients. Classics like cucumber with cream cheese, smoked salmon with dill, and egg and cress sandwiches are presented with artistic flair.

Warm Scones:

Savor the warmth of freshly baked scones, served with clotted cream and strawberry jam. The rich, buttery aroma fills the air as you split open the scone, creating the perfect canvas for the velvety cream and sweet jam.

Sweet Pastries:

Indulge in an array of sweet pastries and cakes displayed on tiered stands. From dainty éclairs to luscious fruit tarts, each bite-sized delicacy is a symphony of textures and flavors, showcasing the pastry chef's artistry.

Devon or Cornish Style:

Embrace the age-old debate of whether to spread jam or cream first on your scone. Choose the Devonshire tradition of cream first, followed by a dollop of jam, or the Cornish method of jam first, topped with cream—each bite is a celebration of personal preference.

Artful Dessert Presentation:

Admire the artful presentation of desserts, where vibrant colors and intricate designs showcase the culinary creativity behind each confection. It's not just a meal; it's a visual feast that elevates the experience.

Variety of Treats:

Appreciate the variety of treats, from dainty macarons to miniature pastries. The assortment caters to a spectrum of tastes, ensuring that every guest finds a sweet indulgence that delights their palate.

Unhurried Enjoyment:

Embrace the unhurried pace of afternoon tea, allowing conversations to flow and moments to linger. The experience is not just about the food; it's about relishing the company, the ambiance, and the sheer pleasure of a leisurely afternoon.

Indulging in traditional afternoon tea is a culinary experience that transcends the ordinary. It's a celebration of refinement, an homage to timeless traditions, and a moment of sheer culinary delight that invites you to savor the artistry of each bite and sip.

TASTE LOCAL CIDERS AND CHEESES

Embarking on a culinary journey to taste local ciders and cheeses is a delightful exploration of regional flavors, craftsmanship, and the rich agricultural heritage of the area. Whether nestled in an orchard or a charming countryside pub, this experience offers a sensory feast that captures the essence of the local terroir.

Orchard Setting:

Begin your tasting adventure in the heart of a picturesque orchard, surrounded by rows of apple and pear trees. The crisp, clean air is infused with the sweet aroma of ripening fruit, setting the stage for an authentic cider experience.

Cider Varieties:

Explore a diverse selection of local ciders, each boasting its unique flavor profile. From traditional dry ciders with a hint of tartness to sweet varieties that burst with fruity notes, the range reflects the orchard's terroir and the cider maker's expertise.

Cider Tasting Flight:

Opt for a cider tasting flight, allowing you to sample an array of flavors. Sip slowly, savoring the nuanced aromas and the dance of flavors on your palate, as each cider tells a story of the orchard's bounty and the cider maker's artistry.

Accompanying Cheeses:

Complement the ciders with a selection of local cheeses, carefully curated to enhance the tasting experience. From creamy brie to tangy cheddar and earthy blue cheeses, each pairing creates a symphony of flavors that elevates both the cider and the cheese.

Pairing Expertise:

Engage with knowledgeable staff or local experts who can guide you through the art of cider and cheese pairing. Their insights into flavor profiles, textures, and regional nuances add a layer of appreciation to each combination.

Countryside Pub Atmosphere:

If you prefer a cozy setting, venture into a countryside pub where the ambiance is warm, and the selection of local ciders and cheeses is curated with care. The pub setting adds a touch of conviviality, inviting you to relax and enjoy the rural charm.

Artisanal Cheese Platter:

Delight in an artisanal cheese platter that showcases the diversity of local dairy craftsmanship. The cheeses may include both cow's milk and sheep's milk varieties, each contributing its unique character to the tasting experience.

Local Orchard Tours:

Consider including a tour of the orchard or cider-making facilities in your experience. Learn about the cider-making process, from the careful selection of apples to the fermentation and bottling stages, gaining a deeper appreciation for the craft.

Seasonal Pairings:

Embrace seasonal pairings by tasting ciders and cheeses that reflect the changing flavors of the orchard and local dairy. Whether it's the bright, crisp ciders of summer or the robust, aged cheeses of winter, each season offers its own palate of delights.

Relaxing Afternoon:

Allow the experience to unfold at a leisurely pace, creating a relaxing afternoon of culinary exploration. Share stories, savor the flavors, and revel in the simple joy of tasting local ciders and cheeses in the heart of the countryside.

Tasting local ciders and cheeses is more than a culinary adventure; it's a celebration of the region's agricultural bounty and the craftsmanship that goes into creating these delectable delights. Each sip and bite tell a story of the land, the people, and the centuries-old traditions that define the local culinary landscape.

EXPERIENCE A COTSWOLD FOOD TOUR

Embarking on a Cotswold food tour is a gastronomic odyssey through charming villages, rolling hills, and local markets, offering a taste of the region's culinary treasures. From artisanal cheeses to farm-fresh produce and delightful pastries, this culinary adventure invites you to savor the flavors that define the Cotswolds.

Market Towns Exploration:

Begin your food tour in one of the Cotswold's market towns, where bustling marketplaces showcase the region's abundance. The lively atmosphere and stalls laden with fresh produce set the stage for a journey into local gastronomy.

Artisanal Bakeries:

Indulge in the aroma of freshly baked goods at artisanal bakeries that line the streets. From crusty loaves of sourdough to delicate pastries filled with local jams, each bite is a testament to the craftsmanship of the bakers who take pride in their creations.

Cheese Tasting:

Immerse yourself in a cheese tasting experience, sampling an array of artisanal cheeses crafted by local producers. From creamy brie to tangy blue varieties, the Cotswolds' rich dairy heritage is on full display, offering a true taste of terroir.

Village Pubs and Inns:

Explore charming village pubs and inns, where traditional Cotswold fare is served with a side of rustic charm. From hearty pies filled with locally sourced ingredients to classic roasts, these establishments provide a cozy setting for culinary exploration.

Local Farm Visits:

Venture to local farms to witness the source of fresh, seasonal produce. Whether it's plucking strawberries from the fields or selecting vegetables straight from the garden, the connection to the land adds depth to your understanding of Cotswold cuisine.

Country Markets:

Stroll through country markets where local producers showcase their goods. From artisanal preserves and chutneys to handmade chocolates and honey, these markets offer a diverse array of culinary delights, each with its own story and flavor.

Cider Orchards:

Explore picturesque cider orchards, where the art of cider making comes to life. Sample a variety of locally crafted ciders, from traditional dry blends to fruit-infused concoctions, while surrounded by the tranquility of the orchard setting.

Tea Rooms with a View:

Pause at quaint tea rooms with panoramic views of the Cotswold landscape. Sip on freshly brewed teas accompanied by delicate sandwiches and pastries, enjoying the combination of culinary indulgence and scenic beauty.

Cooking Workshops:

Participate in cooking workshops led by local chefs, where you can learn to prepare Cotswold-inspired dishes. From mastering traditional recipes to experimenting with modern twists, these workshops add a hands-on dimension to your culinary exploration.

Historic Dining Halls:

Dine in historic dining halls, where the ambiance reflects the Cotswold's timeless allure. Whether it's a meal in a Tudor-era inn or a feast in a centuries-old manor, the historic settings elevate your dining experience, connecting you to the region's rich history.

An authentic Cotswold food tour is not just a culinary journey; it's a celebration of local flavors, culinary heritage, and the sense of community that defines this picturesque region. Each taste is a discovery, and each meal is a chapter in the story of the Cotswolds' vibrant and diverse gastronomic landscape.

COOKING CLASS WITH LOCAL INGREDIENTS

Embark on a delectable journey into the heart of Cotswold cuisine by participating in a cooking class that celebrates the region's rich culinary heritage. Immerse yourself in the world of local flavors and traditional recipes as you engage in a hands-on experience guided by skilled chefs, all while surrounded by the charming ambiance of the Cotswolds.

Choice of Cooking Venue:

Begin your culinary adventure by selecting a picturesque venue for the cooking class. Whether it's a cozy kitchen in a historic inn or a countryside farmhouse, the setting adds an authentic touch to the experience.

Local Chef Expertise:

Benefit from the expertise of a local chef who is well-versed in Cotswold cuisine. Their knowledge of regional ingredients and traditional cooking techniques will serve as a valuable guide throughout the class.

Welcoming Atmosphere:

Step into a welcoming and warm atmosphere as you enter the cooking space. The friendly ambiance encourages camaraderie among participants and sets the stage for a memorable culinary experience.

Introduction to Local Ingredients:

Begin the class with an introduction to the bounty of local ingredients sourced from the Cotswolds. Fresh produce, artisanal cheeses, locally reared meats, and other regional treasures await your culinary exploration.

Hands-On Preparation:

Roll up your sleeves and dive into hands-on preparation. Whether it's crafting the perfect pastry for a Cotswold pie or learning the art of seasoning for a traditional dish, the hands-on approach allows you to truly engage with the culinary process.

Traditional Cotswold Recipes:

Explore the nuances of traditional Cotswold recipes passed down through generations. From hearty stews to delicate desserts, each dish embodies the flavors that define the Cotswolds' gastronomic identity.

Artisanal Cheese Tasting:

Indulge in an artisanal cheese tasting session, featuring some of the finest cheeses produced in the Cotswolds. Learn about the cheese-making process and how these local delights contribute to the region's culinary tapestry.

Guidance on Local Wine Pairing:

Receive guidance on pairing your culinary creations with locally produced wines. Understand the synergy between local dishes and the nuanced flavors of Cotswold wines, enhancing the overall dining experience.

Cooking Techniques and Tips:

Benefit from cooking techniques and tips shared by the local chef. Whether it's mastering the art of rolling out pastry or achieving the perfect sear on locally sourced meat, these insights elevate your culinary skills.

Interactive Cooking Stations:

Engage with interactive cooking stations that allow you to focus on specific aspects of the meal. Whether it's a pasta-making station or a dessert preparation area, the setup ensures a dynamic and immersive experience.

Storytelling and Culinary Traditions:

Immerse yourself in storytelling about culinary traditions and local food customs. Gain insights into the historical significance of certain dishes and the role they play in Cotswold culture.

Communal Dining Experience:

Culminate the cooking class with a communal dining experience. Gather around a beautifully set table with fellow participants to savor the fruits of your labor and share the joy of a meal prepared together.

Recipe Cards for Souvenirs:

Take home more than just memories by receiving recipe cards for the dishes prepared during the class. These souvenirs serve as a tangible connection to the culinary skills and flavors of the Cotswolds.

Culinary Certificates or Diplomas:

Some cooking classes offer culinary certificates or diplomas, recognizing your participation and newfound skills. These certificates become cherished mementos of your culinary adventure in the Cotswolds.

Opportunity for Q&A:

Seize the opportunity for a Q&A session with the local chef. Ask about cooking variations, ingredient substitutions, or any other culinary queries, ensuring you leave the class with enhanced culinary knowledge.

Participating in a cooking class with local ingredients in the Cotswolds is not just a culinary adventure; it's a celebration of flavors, traditions, and the shared joy of preparing and savoring a meal together. As you depart, you carry with you not only new culinary skills but also the essence of Cotswold gastronomy to infuse into your own kitchen.

WINE TASTING IN COTSWOLD VINEYARDS

Embark on a sensory journey through the picturesque landscapes of the Cotswolds as you indulge in a wine tasting experience in the region's esteemed vineyards. Immerse yourself in the art of viticulture, savor the nuanced flavors of locally produced wines, and discover the unique terroir that shapes each vintage. Here's a detailed exploration of what to expect during a wine tasting adventure in the Cotswolds:

Vineyard Selection:

Begin your culinary adventure by selecting a renowned Cotswold vineyard for your wine tasting experience. Choose from a variety of vineyards that showcase the diversity of terroir and grape varietals in the region.

Breathtaking Setting:

Arrive at the vineyard and be captivated by its breathtaking setting. Many Cotswold vineyards are nestled amid rolling hills, offering panoramic views of the countryside that serve as a backdrop to your wine exploration.

Warm Welcome:

Experience a warm welcome from knowledgeable staff or vintners as you enter the vineyard. Their passion for winemaking and the Cotswold landscape enhances your overall wine tasting experience.

Guided Tour of the Vineyard:

Kick off the adventure with a guided tour of the vineyard. Gain insights into the winemaking process, from grape cultivation to harvest, and understand how the unique characteristics of the Cotswolds contribute to the wines' distinct flavors.

Introduction to Grape Varietals:

Delve into the world of grape varietals cultivated in the Cotswolds. From classic varieties like Pinot Noir and Chardonnay to region-specific blends, each grape contributes its own essence to the wines you're about to savor.

Terroir Exploration:

Explore the concept of terroir as it applies to the Cotswold vineyards. Understand how factors such as soil, climate, and altitude influence the character and taste profile of the wines produced in this unique region.

Cellar Tour:

Venture into the vineyard's cellar for an insider's view of the winemaking process. Witness the aging barrels, learn about fermentation techniques, and gain a deeper appreciation for the craftsmanship behind each bottle.

Wine Tasting Flight:

Settle into a charming tasting room or outdoor terrace as you embark on a curated wine tasting flight. Sample a selection of wines, often including whites, reds, and sparkling varieties, allowing you to experience the full spectrum of the vineyard's offerings.

Tasting Notes and Aromas:

Engage your senses as you receive tasting notes from the knowledgeable staff. Explore the aromatic bouquets of each wine, identifying subtle notes of fruits, florals, and spices that contribute to the complexity of the tasting experience.

Food Pairings:

Elevate your tasting with carefully curated food pairings. Local cheeses, artisanal bread, and other culinary delights complement the wines, enhancing the overall sensory experience.

Educational Sessions:

Some vineyards offer educational sessions on wine appreciation. Learn about proper swirling, sniffing, and sipping techniques, empowering you to fully appreciate the intricacies of each pour.

Wine-Making Stories:

Immerse yourself in the stories behind the wines. Vintners often share anecdotes about the challenges and triumphs of winemaking, providing a personal touch to the tasting experience.

Vineyard Events and Festivals:

Check if there are any special events or festivals happening at the vineyard during your visit. Some vineyards host wine-themed gatherings, live music events, or harvest celebrations that add a festive flair to your experience.

Wine Purchases and Souvenirs:

Conclude your wine tasting adventure by perusing the vineyard's shop. Purchase your favorite bottles to savor the Cotswold flavors at home and pick up wine-related souvenirs as lasting reminders of your visit.

Scenic Strolls through the Vineyard:

Take a leisurely stroll through the vineyard grounds after your tasting. Enjoy the beauty of the vine-laden rows, scenic views, and perhaps find a serene spot to relax and absorb the tranquility of the surroundings.

Membership and Wine Clubs:

Explore the possibility of joining the vineyard's wine club or membership program. Many Cotswold vineyards offer exclusive benefits, discounts, and early access to limited releases for their members.

Wine tasting in Cotswold vineyards is not just about sampling exquisite wines; it's an immersive journey that connects you with the region's terroir, traditions, and the artistry of winemaking. From the first sip to the scenic landscapes, each moment unfolds as a celebration of the Cotswolds' rich viticultural heritage.

ATTEND A TRADITIONAL COTSWOLD FEAST

Step into the heart of Cotswold hospitality by partaking in a traditional feast that showcases the region's rich culinary heritage. Immerse yourself in a gastronomic experience where local flavors, time-honored recipes, and conviviality converge to create an unforgettable celebration of Cotswold cuisine.

Venue Selection:

Choose a charming venue that echoes the warmth and authenticity of Cotswold hospitality. Traditional inns, historic manors, or rustic barns often serve as idyllic settings for these feasts.

Welcoming Atmosphere:

Enter the venue to be greeted by a welcoming atmosphere infused with the aromas of Cotswold dishes. The ambiance, whether adorned with rustic decor or classic elegance, sets the stage for a memorable culinary adventure.

Communal Dining Setup:

Find your place at a communal dining table, a hallmark of Cotswold feasting. The shared table fosters a sense of community, encouraging guests to connect over their shared appreciation for good food.

Local Ingredients Showcase:

Feast upon a menu that proudly showcases the bounty of local ingredients sourced from the Cotswolds. From seasonal vegetables to locally reared meats, each dish is a testament to the region's agricultural richness.

Multi-Course Culinary Journey:

Embark on a multi-course culinary journey that unfolds like a story. From appetizers to desserts, each course reveals a different facet of Cotswold gastronomy, allowing you to savor a diverse range of flavors and textures.

Cotswold Aperitifs:

Kick off the feast with traditional Cotswold aperitifs. Local spirits, ales, or cocktails crafted with regional ingredients add a spirited touch to the evening, setting the stage for the culinary delights to come.

Hearty Starters:

Begin with hearty starters that exemplify Cotswold comfort food. Classics such as Scotch eggs, smoked fish, or game terrines pay homage to the region's rustic culinary traditions.

Cotswold Pies and Pastries:

Indulge in Cotswold pies and pastries, each a culinary masterpiece. Whether filled with succulent meats, seasonal vegetables, or creamy cheeses, these creations showcase the artistry of Cotswold bakers.

Roasts and Grilled Specialties:

Delight in succulent roasts and grilled specialties that highlight the region's expertise in preparing meats. Local lamb, beef, or game, expertly seasoned and cooked to perfection, take center stage in this part of the feast.

Seasonal Side Dishes:

Savor seasonal side dishes that complement the main courses. From buttery mashed potatoes to garden-fresh salads, these sides enhance the overall dining experience with their simplicity and freshness.

Local Cheese Board:

Transition to the cheese course with a local cheese board featuring Cotswold varieties. Pair the cheeses with artisanal bread, fruits, and chutneys for a delightful interlude before the dessert course.

Decadent Desserts:

Conclude the feast with decadent desserts that showcase the region's sweet offerings. Traditional puddings, tarts, or desserts featuring locally harvested fruits provide a sweet crescendo to the culinary symphony.

Digestifs and Cordials:

Wind down the feast with Cotswold-inspired digestifs and cordials. Sip on herbal infusions or regional spirits that offer a soothing and flavorful conclusion to the dining experience.

Live Entertainment:

Some traditional Cotswold feasts include live entertainment. Whether it's folk music, storytelling, or performances that celebrate local culture, the entertainment enhances the festive atmosphere of the evening.

Engaging with Locals:

Engage with locals and fellow diners during the feast. Shared laughter, stories, and the joy of discovering new flavors create a sense of camaraderie, making the feast not just a culinary event but a cultural experience.

Recipe Exchanges and Culinary Insights:

Take advantage of the opportunity to exchange recipes and culinary insights with chefs or locals present at the feast. Learn about cooking techniques, ingredient pairings, and the stories behind the beloved dishes served.

Parting Gifts and Souvenirs:

Some feasts offer parting gifts or souvenirs to commemorate the experience. This could range from recipe booklets to locally crafted items, allowing you to carry a piece of the Cotswolds back with you.

Attending a traditional Cotswold feast is not merely a dining experience; it's a cultural immersion where the flavors, stories, and conviviality of the region come together. As you leave the feast, you carry not only the taste of Cotswold dishes but also the warmth of shared moments and the richness of a culinary heritage deeply rooted in the heart of the countryside.

FESTIVALS AND EVENTS

ATTEND THE CHELTENHAM LITERATURE FESTIVAL

Embark on a literary adventure in the charming town of Cheltenham as you attend the renowned Cheltenham Literature Festival. This annual celebration of literature draws book lovers, authors, and thinkers from around the world, offering a captivating blend of literary discussions, author events, and cultural experiences that enrich the mind and soul.

Historic Venue Setting:

Enter the historic venues that serve as the backdrop for the Cheltenham Literature Festival. The festival's events unfold in iconic spaces, from grand theaters to intimate literary salons, creating an atmosphere that resonates with the town's rich cultural heritage.

Literary Buzz and Energy:

Immerse yourself in the vibrant buzz and energy that permeate the festival. As you approach the venues, the excitement of fellow literature enthusiasts and the anticipation of intellectual exploration create a palpable sense of community and shared passion.

Diverse Author Lineup:

Explore the diverse lineup of authors who grace the Cheltenham Literature Festival stages. From acclaimed novelists to thought-provoking poets, the festival curates a spectrum of voices, ensuring a rich tapestry of literary perspectives and genres.

Author Talks and Panel Discussions:

Attend author talks and panel discussions that delve into the minds and inspirations of literary giants. Engage with the thought-provoking conversations as authors share insights into their creative processes, the themes of their works, and the broader cultural landscapes that influence their writing.

Literary Salons and Intimate Gatherings:

Delve into literary salons and intimate gatherings that offer a more personal connection with authors. These smaller settings provide an opportunity for in-depth discussions, allowing attendees to interact with their favorite writers on a more personal level.

Book Readings and Storytelling Sessions:

Experience the magic of book readings and storytelling sessions that transport you into the worlds created by words. From the cadence of poetry to the narrative prose of novels, these sessions allow you to connect with the essence of storytelling.

Poetry Slams and Spoken Word Performances:

Engage in the rhythm and power of poetry slams and spoken word performances. The festival celebrates the spoken word as poets take the stage, weaving narratives and emotions through their verses in performances that captivate and inspire.

Book Signings and Meet-the-Author Events:

Attend book signings and meet-the-author events, where you have the chance to interact with your literary heroes. Personalize your reading collection as authors inscribe their works, creating cherished mementos of your festival experience.

Literary Workshops and Masterclasses:

Participate in literary workshops and masterclasses that offer a hands-on exploration of the craft. Whether it's honing your writing skills, understanding the nuances of storytelling, or delving into the intricacies of poetry, these sessions cater to both aspiring and established writers.

Cultural Exchange and Global Perspectives:

Immerse yourself in cultural exchange and global perspectives as the Cheltenham Literature Festival attracts authors and speakers from diverse backgrounds and corners of the world. The festival becomes a meeting point for ideas, fostering cross-cultural dialogue and understanding.

Interactive Exhibitions and Installations:

Explore interactive exhibitions and installations that add a multi-sensory dimension to the literary experience. From immersive displays of literary history to art installations inspired by classic works, these elements enrich your festival journey.

Book Market and Independent Bookshops:

Roam through the bustling book market and independent bookshops that surround the festival venues. Discover hidden gems, rare editions, and the latest releases as you browse through the literary offerings that spill onto the streets.

Literary Fringe Events and Street Performances:

Immerse yourself in the literary fringe events and street performances that spill onto the festival's periphery. The streets of Cheltenham come alive with artistic expression, creating an atmosphere where literature blends seamlessly with the town's vibrant culture.

Evening Gala Events and Celebrations:

Conclude your days at the Cheltenham Literature Festival with evening gala events and celebrations. From awards ceremonies to cultural soirées, these gatherings provide a festive culmination to each day, allowing attendees to revel in the shared joy of literary exploration.

Attending the Cheltenham Literature Festival is not just an event; it's an enriching journey into the world of words, ideas, and the transformative power of literature. The festival becomes a meeting ground for minds, a celebration of creativity, and a testament to the enduring magic of storytelling in the heart of the picturesque town of Cheltenham.

JOIN THE COTSWOLD LAVENDER HARVEST

Step into a fragrant tapestry of purple hues as you embark on a sensory journey during the Cotswold Lavender Harvest. This annual event invites visitors to immerse themselves in the beauty of lavender fields, experience the harvesting process, and revel in the therapeutic and picturesque landscapes of the Cotswolds.

Entrance to Lavender Fields:

Begin your Lavender Harvest experience by entering the expansive lavender fields. The entrance welcomes you with the gentle hum of bees and the captivating sight of rows upon rows of blooming lavender, creating a symphony of color and scent.

Aromatic Bouquet in the Air:

As you step further into the fields, the air becomes infused with the sweet and aromatic fragrance of lavender. Inhale deeply, and let the calming scent transport you into a world of serenity and natural beauty.

Endless Purple Vistas:

Marvel at the endless vistas of purple stretching out before you. The neatly arranged lavender rows create a mesmerizing visual display, forming a striking contrast against the greenery of the surrounding landscape.

Varieties of Lavender:

Explore the diverse varieties of lavender cultivated in the fields. From English Lavender (Lavandula angustifolia) to French Lavender (Lavandula stoechas), each variety adds its unique charm and characteristics to the overall tapestry of the lavender landscape.

Harvesting Demonstrations:

Engage in harvesting demonstrations led by knowledgeable guides. Learn about the different methods of harvesting lavender, from traditional hand-cutting to modern machinery, and gain insights into the various uses of harvested lavender.

Hands-On Harvesting Experience:

Take part in the hands-on harvesting experience. Armed with scissors, immerse yourself in the act of carefully cutting lavender stems. Feel the softness of the lavender in your hands and appreciate the meditative quality of this timeless agricultural tradition.

Lavender Distillation Process:

Discover the lavender distillation process as guides explain how essential oils are extracted from the harvested lavender. Witness the distillation equipment in action and learn about the aromatic properties that make lavender essential oil highly prized.

Lavender Products Showcase:

Visit showcases featuring an array of lavender-based products. From essential oils and sachets to lavender-infused culinary delights, these displays highlight the versatility of lavender and offer an opportunity to take home a piece of the harvest.

Lavender-Infused Refreshments:

Indulge in lavender-infused refreshments at designated areas within the fields. Sip on lavender lemonade, enjoy lavender-flavored ice cream, or partake in other culinary delights that incorporate the essence of this aromatic herb.

Artistic Photo Opportunities:

Seize artistic photo opportunities amidst the lavender fields. Capture the interplay of light and shadow, the vivid purples against the blue sky, and the delicate details of lavender blooms. The fields become a natural canvas for photography enthusiasts.

Relaxation Areas and Picnic Spots:

Unwind in designated relaxation areas and picnic spots scattered throughout the lavender fields. Bring a blanket, enjoy a leisurely picnic, and soak in the tranquil ambiance surrounded by the beauty of nature.

Children's Activities and Entertainment:

Engage in children's activities and entertainment for a family-friendly experience. From lavender-themed crafts to storytelling sessions, the event caters to visitors of all ages, ensuring a delightful day out for families.

Live Music and Performances:

Immerse yourself in the enchanting atmosphere enhanced by live music and performances. Local musicians and artists add a melodic backdrop to the Lavender Harvest, creating an ambiance that complements the natural beauty of the surroundings.

Sunset Lavender Walks:

Conclude your day with sunset lavender walks, where the fading sunlight bathes the fields in a warm glow. The changing colors of the sky provide a breathtaking backdrop as you stroll through the lavender, creating a magical and serene conclusion to your Lavender Harvest experience.

Joining the Cotswold Lavender Harvest is not just a festival; it's a celebration of nature's beauty, the timeless tradition of lavender cultivation, and the therapeutic essence that permeates the lavender fields. It offers a sensory retreat, inviting visitors to connect with the natural wonders of the Cotswolds in a truly enchanting setting.

CELEBRATE THE PAINSWICK ROCOCO GARDEN SNOWDROP WEEK

Step into a winter wonderland of delicate blooms as you join the enchanting celebration of Snowdrop Week at the Painswick Rococo Garden. This annual event transforms the historic garden into a tapestry of white, where the beauty of snowdrops takes center stage, heralding the arrival of spring in the heart of the Cotswolds.

Entrance to Rococo Garden:

Begin your Snowdrop Week adventure by entering the gates of the Painswick Rococo Garden. The historic surroundings, framed by stone walls and ancient trees, set the stage for a captivating journey through a landscape adorned with nature's delicate jewels.

Snowdrop-Covered Pathways:

Wander along pathways adorned with a blanket of snowdrops. The pristine white blooms create a striking contrast against the greenery, transforming the garden into a serene and magical realm that captivates the senses.

Varieties of Snowdrops:

Discover the diverse varieties of snowdrops that grace the Rococo Garden. From the classic Galanthus nivalis to unique cultivars, each variety contributes to the intricate tapestry of white, showcasing the beauty and diversity of these early spring flowers.

Snowdrop Displays and Collections:

Encounter carefully curated displays and collections of snowdrops strategically placed throughout the garden. These showcases highlight specific varieties, allowing visitors to appreciate the subtle nuances in size, shape, and markings that make each snowdrop unique.

Snowdrop Walks and Guided Tours:

Engage in snowdrop walks and guided tours led by knowledgeable garden guides. Learn about the history and significance of snowdrops, their natural habitats, and the horticultural practices employed in the Rococo Garden to cultivate and showcase these delicate winter blooms.

Snowdrop Photography Opportunities:

Seize enchanting photography opportunities amidst the snowdrops. Capture the delicate details of individual blooms, explore creative angles, and document the landscape as it transforms into a sea of white petals, creating a visual spectacle for photography enthusiasts.

Historic Garden Features:

Appreciate the integration of snowdrops with the Rococo Garden's historic features. From the ornate follies to the architectural elements, the snowdrops add a touch of ephemeral beauty, creating a harmonious blend of historical charm and natural elegance.

Snowdrop-Themed Art Installations:

Encounter snowdrop-themed art installations that add an artistic dimension to the garden. Sculptures, installations, and ephemeral creations celebrate the beauty of snowdrops and enhance the overall sensory experience.

Winter Wildlife Observations:

Observe winter wildlife that thrives in the garden during Snowdrop Week. From birds seeking shelter to glimpses of early pollinators, the garden becomes a haven for nature enthusiasts keen on exploring the delicate balance between flora and fauna in the winter months.

Snowdrop-Themed Workshops:

Participate in snowdrop-themed workshops that offer hands-on experiences. From botanical art classes to horticultural demonstrations, these workshops provide insights into the cultivation and appreciation of snowdrops.

Hot Beverages and Refreshments:

Take a break at designated areas offering hot beverages and refreshments. Warm up with a cup of hot tea or coffee, surrounded by the serene beauty of snowdrops, creating a cozy interlude in your exploration of the winter garden.

Winter Garden Picnics:

Bring a winter picnic and savor seasonal treats amidst the snowdrops. Designated picnic areas allow visitors to enjoy the tranquil ambiance while relishing the crisp air and the company of friends and family.

Live Music and Winter Performances:

Immerse yourself in the festive atmosphere enhanced by live music and winter performances. Local musicians and performers contribute to the joyful ambiance, creating an enchanting backdrop for your Snowdrop Week celebrations.

Snowdrop-Themed Souvenirs:

Conclude your visit by exploring snowdrop-themed souvenirs at the garden's gift shop. From botanical prints to snowdrop bulbs, these mementos offer a way to extend the magic of Snowdrop Week beyond your garden exploration.

Celebrate the Painswick Rococo Garden Snowdrop Week as more than an event; it's a journey into the delicate beauty of winter blooms and the timeless charm of one of the Cotswolds' most enchanting gardens. The Rococo Garden becomes a canvas of natural artistry, inviting visitors to revel in the ephemeral splendor of snowdrops and embrace the promise of spring on the horizon.

OUTDOOR ADVENTURES

HOT AIR BALLOON RIDE OVER THE COUNTRYSIDE

Embarking on a hot air balloon ride over the Cotswold countryside is a breathtaking outdoor adventure that unveils the region's panoramic beauty from a unique vantage point. Drifting gently above rolling hills, picturesque villages, and meandering rivers, this experience offers a sense of tranquility and awe as you become one with the skies.

Preparation and Liftoff:

The adventure begins with the inflation of the hot air balloon at dawn or dusk, creating a captivating scene of billowing fabric against the backdrop of the Cotswold landscape. As the balloon gently rises, the anticipation builds, and the countryside unfolds beneath you.

Bird's-Eye View of Villages:

Soar above charming Cotswold villages with their honey-hued stone cottages and labyrinthine streets. From the elevated perspective of the balloon basket, the villages take on a miniature quality, and the architectural details become even more enchanting.

Rolling Hills and Farmlands:

Glide over the undulating landscapes of the Cotswold Hills, where fields of green and gold stretch out to the horizon. The patchwork quilt of farmlands, hedgerows, and meadows unfolds beneath you, creating a mesmerizing vista that captures the essence of rural England.

Tranquil Rivers and Streams:

Drift gracefully over tranquil rivers and streams that meander through the countryside. The reflective surface of the water mirrors the surrounding landscape, adding a serene and poetic quality to the journey.

Wildlife Encounters:

Experience wildlife encounters from a bird's-eye view. Spot deer grazing in fields, birds soaring in the thermals, and the occasional glimpse of foxes or hares as you float silently through the air. The peacefulness of the balloon ride minimizes your impact on the natural surroundings, allowing for unobtrusive wildlife observation.

Cotswold Stone Architecture:

Marvel at the Cotswold stone architecture from an elevated perspective. The intricate details of manor houses, churches, and historic landmarks become more apparent, providing a newfound appreciation for the craftsmanship of these structures.

Autumn Colors and Harvest Fields:

During the autumn season, witness the Cotswolds adorned in a tapestry of warm hues. The golden glow of harvest fields, the fiery reds of turning leaves, and the amber sunlight casting long shadows create a magical and evocative atmosphere.

Photographic Opportunities:

Capture stunning photographs as the changing light of sunrise or sunset bathes the landscape in a soft, golden glow. The panoramic views offer endless opportunities for capturing the beauty of the Cotswolds from a perspective seldom seen.

Gentle Breeze and Silence:

Experience the gentle breeze and the sensation of weightlessness as the balloon drifts silently through the air. The absence of engine noise allows for a serene and meditative journey, creating a profound connection with the natural surroundings.

Champagne Toast and Landing:

Conclude the adventure with a traditional champagne toast upon landing. Celebrate the exhilarating experience as you share stories with fellow adventurers and the crew. The balloon's descent marks the end of an unforgettable journey through the skies.

A hot air balloon ride over the Cotswold countryside is more than an outdoor adventure; it's a poetic and immersive experience that allows you to see the world below in a new light. The tranquility, the breathtaking views, and the sense of floating above the patchwork beauty of the Cotswolds create memories that linger long after the balloon touches down.

HORSEBACK RIDING IN THE COTSWOLD HILLS

Embarking on a horseback riding adventure in the Cotswold Hills is a thrilling journey through bucolic landscapes, ancient bridleways, and quaint villages. Mounted on a majestic horse, you become one with the rolling hills, meadows, and woodland paths, immersing yourself in the natural beauty and timeless charm of the Cotswolds.

Riding Center Welcome:

Begin your adventure at a reputable horseback riding center nestled in the heart of the Cotswold Hills. Here, seasoned guides and well-trained horses await, ensuring a safe and enjoyable experience for riders of all levels.

Meet Your Equine Companion:

Form a connection with your equine companion as you meet, groom, and saddle up your horse. The bond between rider and horse is integral to the experience, creating a sense of trust and partnership for the journey ahead.

Cotswold Trail Exploration:

Set out on a trail that winds through the undulating landscapes of the Cotswold Hills. The rhythmic clip-clop of hooves on ancient bridleways and quiet lanes sets the pace for an adventure that unfolds at a leisurely canter.

Panoramic Hilltop Views:

Ascend to hilltop vantage points that offer panoramic views of the surrounding countryside. The Cotswold Hills reveal their splendor as you look out over patchwork fields, historic landmarks, and charming villages nestled in the valleys below.

Bridleways and Woodland Paths:

Traverse bridleways that crisscross the landscape, taking you through ancient woodlands and along meandering streams. The diversity of the terrain adds excitement to the ride, with each turn offering a new vista to explore.

Charming Village Routes:

Ride through quaint Cotswold villages, where narrow lanes and honey-colored stone cottages transport you to a bygone era. The horse's gentle gait allows you to absorb the picturesque scenes at a leisurely pace, providing an authentic experience of rural life.

Seasonal Beauty:

Experience the changing seasons as you ride through meadows adorned with wildflowers in spring, shaded woodlands in summer, golden fields in autumn, and frost-kissed landscapes in winter. Each season brings its own enchantment to the Cotswold countryside.

Guided Historical Narratives:

Benefit from the expertise of knowledgeable guides who share historical narratives and local lore along the way. Learn about the rich heritage of the Cotswolds, from ancient settlements to tales of bygone equestrian traditions.

Wildlife Encounters:

Encounter local wildlife such as deer, rabbits, and a variety of bird species as you ride through natural habitats. The gentle approach of horses often allows for close wildlife observation without disturbing the natural rhythms of the environment.

Picnic Stopovers:

Enjoy picnic stopovers in scenic locations, where you can dismount, relax, and savor a locally sourced picnic. The peaceful moments spent amidst nature and your equine companions add a leisurely and immersive aspect to the horseback riding experience.

Sunset Rides:

Opt for a sunset ride, where the warm hues of the evening sky cast a magical glow over the Cotswold Hills. The fading sunlight creates an atmospheric backdrop, turning the adventure into a serene and memorable twilight experience.

Return to Riding Center:

Conclude your horseback riding adventure with a return to the riding center. As you dismount and bid farewell to your four-legged friend, reflect on the unique perspective gained and the indelible memories created during your journey through the Cotswold Hills.

Horseback riding in the Cotswold Hills is more than a physical activity; it's an immersive encounter with nature, history, and the timeless beauty of the English countryside. Whether you're a novice rider or an experienced equestrian, the Cotswold Hills offer an enchanting canvas for a horseback adventure that leaves a lasting imprint on your spirit.

KAYAKING ON THE RIVER THAMES

Embarking on a kayaking adventure on the River Thames is a dynamic exploration of England's iconic waterway, offering a unique perspective on historic landmarks, serene landscapes, and the gentle flow of the river. Paddling along the Thames provides a blend of tranquility and excitement, allowing you to connect with nature and witness the beauty of the surrounding countryside.

Kayaking Center Orientation:

Begin your adventure at a reputable kayaking center along the River Thames. Here, experienced guides provide safety briefings, equipment orientation, and paddling instructions, ensuring that both beginners and experienced kayakers are well-prepared for the journey ahead.

Launch Point:

Set off from a designated launch point, where the gentle ripples of the Thames invite you to dip your paddle into its waters. The initial strokes signal the beginning of a journey that meanders through both urban and rural landscapes.

Cityscape Paddling:

Navigate through urban stretches of the Thames, passing iconic landmarks such as the Tower Bridge and the Shard. The juxtaposition of modern architecture against the historic river creates a captivating contrast, providing a kayaking experience unlike any other.

Historic Riverside Views:

Paddle past historic riverside sites, including the Tower of London and St. Paul's Cathedral. The waterborne perspective offers a unique angle to appreciate the grandeur of these landmarks, with their intricate details and architectural splendor.

Tree-Lined Stretches:

Explore tree-lined stretches of the Thames, where the overhanging branches create a canopy of greenery. These tranquil sections provide a respite from the urban bustle, allowing you to immerse yourself in the natural beauty of the riverbanks.

Wildlife Encounters:

Witness wildlife along the riverbanks, from swans gracefully gliding on the water to ducks and geese foraging along the shore. The Thames is a haven for birdlife, and the peaceful passage of a kayak allows for unobtrusive observation of these aquatic habitats.

Riverside Villages:

Paddle past charming riverside villages with their historic cottages and waterside pubs. The rhythmic sound of paddles complements the timeless ambiance, creating a picturesque scene that invites exploration and appreciation of riverside communities.

River Islands and Oxbows:

Navigate around river islands and explore oxbows, where the meandering course of the Thames unveils hidden corners and peaceful alcoves. These natural features add an element of discovery to your kayaking journey.

Picnic Stopovers:

Take advantage of designated picnic spots along the riverbanks. Pull your kayak ashore, enjoy a riverside picnic, and soak in the beauty of the surrounding landscape. The Thames becomes a tranquil haven for relaxation and contemplation.

Lock Navigation:

Encounter historic river locks, where the water levels change to facilitate navigation. The teamwork involved in paddling through locks adds an interactive element to the kayaking experience, providing insight into the engineering marvels of the Thames.

Sunset Paddling:

Opt for a sunset kayaking excursion, where the warm hues of the setting sun reflect on the water's surface. The serene twilight ambiance adds a magical quality to the journey, transforming the river into a canvas of colors.

Riverside Pub Landings:

Conclude your kayaking adventure with landings near riverside pubs. Enjoy a well-deserved meal or refreshments as you recount the highlights of your journey with fellow paddlers, creating a convivial ending to your day on the Thames.

Kayaking on the River Thames is a multisensory adventure that blends the thrill of paddling with the serenity of the waterway. Whether you're captivated by urban vistas or enchanted by the tranquility of rural stretches, the Thames offers a diverse and immersive kayaking experience that reveals the river's timeless allure.

CYCLING EXPLORATION

BIKE THE COTSWOLD CYCLE ROUTE

Embark on an exhilarating cycling adventure through the timeless beauty of the Cotswolds by exploring the renowned Cotswold Cycle Route. This scenic journey takes you through charming villages, rolling hills, and bucolic landscapes, offering a perfect blend of outdoor activity and immersion into the quintessential charm of the English countryside.

Starting Point:

Begin your cycling exploration at a designated starting point, often marked by a trailhead or a prominent location. Make sure your bike is in top condition, and don't forget essentials like a helmet, water, and a map.

Picturesque Villages:

Pedal through picturesque Cotswold villages that seem frozen in time. Quaint stone cottages, thatched roofs, and vibrant flower gardens create a postcard-perfect setting as you navigate the narrow lanes of charming locales.

Scenic Countryside Views:

Revel in the panoramic views of the Cotswold countryside as you traverse rolling hills and verdant meadows. Each turn in the route reveals a new vista, with patchwork fields, hedgerows, and distant hills forming a captivating landscape.

Cotswold Stone Architecture:

Appreciate the timeless allure of Cotswold stone architecture. Churches, manor houses, and historic landmarks showcase the region's distinctive honey-colored stone, creating a harmonious blend with the natural surroundings.

Winding Country Lanes:

Follow winding country lanes that lead you deeper into the heart of the Cotswolds. These scenic routes, bordered by hedgerows and dotted with wildflowers, offer an intimate connection with the tranquil beauty of the countryside.

Cotswold Way Trail Sections:

Encounter sections of the Cotswold Way trail during your cycling journey. This long-distance footpath traverses the Cotswolds, providing opportunities to explore wooded areas, hilltops, and ancient sites along the way.

Quirky Cotswold Gardens:

Discover hidden gems like quirky Cotswold gardens that invite you to take a break. Some routes may pass by renowned gardens where you can pause to admire the blooms, relax in a tranquil setting, and perhaps enjoy a picnic.

Local Pubs and Tea Houses:

Plan pit stops at local pubs or tea houses along the route. These charming establishments offer a taste of Cotswold hospitality, with hearty meals, traditional afternoon teas, and a chance to interact with locals.

Cotswold Wildlife Encounters:

Keep an eye out for Cotswold wildlife as you cycle through the countryside. Deer, hares, and a variety of bird species may make appearances, adding a touch of nature's magic to your cycling adventure.

Historic Market Towns:

Explore historic market towns nestled along the cycle route. Market squares, medieval architecture, and bustling streets provide opportunities to delve into the Cotswolds' rich history and perhaps indulge in some local shopping.

Elevated Viewpoints:

Climb to elevated viewpoints along the route for breathtaking panoramic vistas. Hilltops and viewpoints such as Broadway Tower or Dover's Hill offer a sense of achievement and reward you with sweeping views of the surrounding countryside.

Cotswold Waterways:

Encounter Cotswold waterways, be it gentle streams, rivers, or serene lakes. Cycling alongside these waterways offers moments of tranquility and a chance to appreciate the reflections of the Cotswold landscape.

Cotswold Festivals and Events:

Check the local calendar for Cotswold festivals or events taking place during your ride. Whether it's a village fair, a traditional celebration, or a cycling event, joining in adds a festive and communal element to your exploration.

Guided Cycling Tours:

Consider joining guided cycling tours led by local experts. These tours provide insights into the region's history, ecology, and folklore, enhancing your overall understanding of the Cotswolds.

Seasonal Cycling Experiences:

Tailor your cycling exploration to the seasons. Spring brings blooming wildflowers, summer offers lush greenery, autumn showcases vibrant foliage, and winter provides a crisp and serene atmosphere.

Local Artisanal Stops:

Visit local artisanal stops along the route. Whether it's a pottery studio, craft shop, or a farm offering fresh produce, these stops allow you to connect with the creative spirit of the Cotswolds.

End with a Cotswold Cream Tea:

Conclude your cycling adventure with a quintessential Cotswold cream tea. Find a cozy tearoom, indulge in scones with clotted cream and jam, and savor the satisfaction of a day well spent exploring the Cotswold Cycle Route.

Biking the Cotswold Cycle Route is not just a physical activity; it's a journey that immerses you in the timeless beauty and cultural richness of the Cotswolds. Whether you're a seasoned cyclist or a leisure rider, this exploration promises an enchanting encounter with the picturesque landscapes and storied heritage of this cherished region.

MOUNTAIN BIKING IN CRANHAM WOODS

Embark on an adrenaline-fueled adventure as you explore the exhilarating trails of Cranham Woods on a mountain biking expedition. Nestled within the Cotswolds, Cranham Woods offers an immersive experience for avid mountain bikers, combining technical challenges, natural beauty, and a sense of adventure.

Here's a detailed exploration of what awaits you on this thrilling cycling journey:

Trailhead Entry:

Begin your mountain biking expedition at the trailhead of Cranham Woods. The entrance sets the tone for the adventure ahead, surrounded by the tranquility of the woodland and the promise of exciting trails.

Technical Singletracks:

Navigate through technical singletracks that wind their way through the woods. These trails, designed to challenge your biking skills, feature twists, turns, and varying elevations, providing an engaging and dynamic riding experience.

Woodland Canopy Ride:

Enjoy a canopy ride through the dense woodland. Tall trees create a natural tunnel, casting dappled sunlight on the trail, and offering a thrilling sense of being immersed in nature as you speed through the forest.

Natural Obstacles:

Encounter natural obstacles such as roots, rocks, and fallen logs that add an extra layer of challenge to the trails. Negotiate these features with skill, enhancing the technical aspect of your mountain biking experience.

Downhill Descents:

Experience adrenaline-pumping downhill descents that reward you with bursts of speed. Cranham Woods' varied terrain provides opportunities for exhilarating descents, offering a thrilling contrast to the climbs.

Uphill Challenges:

Conquer uphill challenges that test your endurance and strength. Cranham Woods' trails include ascents that require determination, providing a satisfying workout for mountain bikers seeking both thrills and physical exertion.

Scenic Clearings and Views:

Discover scenic clearings within the woods that offer breathtaking views of the surrounding landscape. Pause to absorb the beauty of the Cotswold countryside, creating moments of serenity amid the excitement of your ride.

Berm Turns and Banked Corners:

Navigate bermed turns and banked corners strategically incorporated into the trails. These features not only add a fun and dynamic element to your ride but also showcase the thoughtful design of the mountain biking routes.

Hidden Trails and Exploration:

Explore hidden trails that veer off the main paths, inviting you to discover secluded pockets of Cranham Woods. These trails may lead to unexpected clearings, viewpoints, or natural features, adding an element of exploration to your adventure.

Technical Trail Features:

Encounter technical trail features such as rock gardens, jumps, and drop-offs. Cranham Woods caters to riders seeking an elevated level of challenge, providing opportunities to test and improve your mountain biking skills.

Seasonal Changes:

Embrace the seasonal changes in Cranham Woods. Spring brings blossoming flowers and vibrant greenery, summer offers dense foliage, autumn showcases a riot of colors, and winter provides a crisp and invigorating atmosphere.

Wildlife Sightings:

Keep an eye out for wildlife during your mountain biking journey. Deer, squirrels, and a variety of bird species may make appearances, adding a touch of nature's wonder to your trail experience.

Trail Etiquette:

Adhere to trail etiquette and respect fellow riders. Cranham Woods may attract mountain biking enthusiasts of various skill levels, and maintaining courtesy ensures a positive and enjoyable experience for everyone.

Technical Skills Area:

Seek out a dedicated technical skills area if available. These areas often feature man-made obstacles like ramps, drops, and balance features, providing a space for riders to hone their skills before tackling more challenging trails.

Trail Markers and Maps:

Utilize trail markers and maps to navigate the expansive network of trails in Cranham Woods. Clear signage ensures you stay on course, and maps offer insights into the variety of trails and their difficulty levels.

Maintenance and Preservation:

Participate in trail maintenance and preservation efforts. Many mountain biking communities contribute to keeping trails in optimal condition, and your involvement ensures that future riders can enjoy Cranham Woods in its pristine state.

Post-Ride Refreshments:

Conclude your mountain biking adventure with well-deserved post-ride refreshments. Whether it's a packed picnic or a visit to a local cafe, relish the satisfaction of conquering Cranham Woods' trails and share tales of your biking exploits.

Mountain biking in Cranham Woods transcends the ordinary ride—it's an immersive journey through challenging terrain, natural beauty, and the thrill of exploration. As you navigate the trails, each twist and turn becomes a testament to the dynamic allure of mountain biking in one of the Cotswolds' hidden gems.

GUIDED CYCLING TOUR THROUGH QUAINT VILLAGES

Embark on a leisurely and informative guided cycling tour that takes you through the enchanting landscape of the Cotswolds, weaving through quaint villages steeped in history and charm. This guided experience offers a perfect blend of cycling, storytelling, and exploration, providing you with an intimate connection to the timeless beauty of the English countryside.

Meet Your Local Guide:

Begin your cycling adventure by meeting your knowledgeable local guide. Their expertise in the region's history, architecture, and hidden gems adds depth to your journey as they share insights and anecdotes throughout the tour.

Bike Fitting and Safety Briefing:

Ensure a comfortable ride by having your bike fitted to your specifications. Your guide provides a safety briefing, ensuring that everyone is equipped with helmets and understands the rules of the road for a secure and enjoyable cycling experience.

Quaint Village Starting Point:

Start your tour from a quaint village that serves as the perfect launchpad for your exploration. The village's character and charm set the stage for the scenic ride ahead.

Storybook Cottages and Thatched Roofs:

Pedal through lanes lined with storybook cottages adorned with thatched roofs. Your guide shares stories about the architectural history of these dwellings, creating a visual and narrative feast as you cycle through.

Historic Churches and Landmarks:

Visit historic churches and landmarks scattered throughout the villages. Your guide provides insights into the significance of these structures, highlighting their architectural features and the role they played in local history.

Hidden Alleyways and Pathways:

Explore hidden alleyways and pathways that unveil the quieter and less-traveled corners of the villages. These charming passages often lead to unexpected treasures, inviting you to discover the village's nuances beyond the main thoroughfares.

Local Artisans and Craftsmen:

Stop at workshops and studios of local artisans and craftsmen. Your guide introduces you to the creative spirit of the Cotswolds, whether it's a pottery studio, a blacksmith's forge, or a craftsman producing handmade goods.

Tea Houses and Traditional Inns:

Take a break at tea houses and traditional inns along the route. Your guide may recommend local specialties, and you can savor a cup of tea or indulge in a light snack, soaking in the ambiance of these quintessentially English establishments.

Guided Stories of Village Life:

Engage in guided stories about village life past and present. Your guide shares tales of local characters, historical events, and the unique traditions that contribute to the identity of each village.

Seasonal Highlights:

Appreciate seasonal highlights as your cycling tour unfolds. Whether it's blooming flowers in spring, vibrant foliage in autumn, or festive decorations during the holidays, each season brings its own magical touch to the villages.

Encounters with Locals:

Interact with locals as you cycle through the villages. Your guide may facilitate conversations with residents, providing you with a firsthand perspective on daily life and the close-knit community spirit that defines Cotswold villages.

Village Greens and Market Squares:

Pause at village greens and market squares that serve as central gathering points. Learn about the history of markets, festivals, and community events that have taken place in these lively hubs.

Guided Interpretation of Architecture:

Receive a guided interpretation of architectural styles prevalent in the villages. From medieval timber-framed houses to Georgian and Victorian structures, your guide elucidates the evolution of architectural aesthetics in the Cotswolds.

Village Pond Reflections:

Admire reflections in village ponds, adding a tranquil and picturesque element to your tour. These serene spots offer a chance to pause, reflect, and capture the timeless beauty of the Cotswolds.

Customizable Routes:

Enjoy a tour with customizable routes based on your preferences and interests. Your guide may tailor the itinerary to include specific attractions or cater to the group's pace, ensuring a personalized and enjoyable experience.

Hidden Gardens and Secret Spaces:

Discover hidden gardens and secret spaces tucked away in the villages. Your guide unveils these quiet retreats, allowing you to immerse yourself in the beauty of carefully tended flora and escape the bustle of the main streets.

Culinary Delights and Local Fare:

Conclude your guided cycling tour with a taste of local culinary delights. Your guide may recommend a charming tearoom or a traditional pub, providing an opportunity to savor Cotswold fare and toast to the success of your village exploration.

A guided cycling tour through quaint villages is not just a physical journey; it's a cultural and historical immersion into the essence of the Cotswolds. As you pedal through these charming locales, guided by the stories and expertise of a local, each village becomes a chapter in a captivating narrative that unfolds against the backdrop of timeless beauty and rural tranquility.

WINTER WONDERLAND

CHRISTMAS MARKET MAGIC IN BATH

Step into a festive dreamscape with the enchanting "Christmas Market Magic in Bath." Set against the backdrop of historic architecture and cobbled streets, this winter wonderland experience immerses visitors in the magical ambiance of one of England's most celebrated Christmas markets.

Grand Entrance to the Christmas Market:

Begin your magical journey with a grand entrance to the Christmas market. Walk through beautifully adorned archways, guided by the warm glow of festive lights that herald the entrance to a world of holiday cheer. The scent of mulled wine and seasonal treats fills the air, creating an immediate sense of festive anticipation.

Festive Stalls and Boutique Shops:

Explore a myriad of festive stalls and boutique shops adorned with twinkling lights and tasteful decorations. Each stall is a treasure trove of handcrafted gifts, festive ornaments, and artisanal delights. Visitors can meander through the stalls, discovering unique and locally crafted items that make for perfect holiday gifts.

Traditional Christmas Market Chalets:

Wander through traditional Christmas market chalets, each exuding a cozy and inviting atmosphere. These chalets showcase a charming array of handmade crafts, delicate decorations, and seasonal treats. The festive decorations create a picture-perfect scene, transporting visitors to a winter wonderland reminiscent of a holiday fairy tale.

Mulled Wine and Festive Treats:

Indulge in the quintessential winter experience of sipping warm mulled wine while strolling through the market. The aroma of cinnamon and spices wafts through the air as visitors enjoy festive treats like roasted chestnuts, gingerbread cookies, and other delectable seasonal specialties.

Live Carolers and Festive Music:

Immerse yourself in the joyous sounds of live carolers and festive music that echo through the market square. Enchanting melodies fill the air, creating a harmonious backdrop to the joyful atmosphere. Visitors can join in the festive spirit by singing along or simply basking in the heartwarming tunes.

Santa's Grotto for the Little Ones:

Create magical memories for the little ones with a visit to Santa's Grotto. Nestled in a charming corner of the market, the grotto is adorned with twinkling lights and festive decor. Children have the opportunity to meet Santa, share their Christmas wishes, and receive a small token of holiday joy.

Ferris Wheel with Panoramic Views:

Take a ride on the Ferris wheel for panoramic views of the Christmas market and the charming city of Bath adorned in festive lights. The Ferris wheel becomes a dazzling centerpiece, offering visitors a unique vantage point to admire the festive decorations, bustling stalls, and the winter wonderland that unfolds beneath.

Ice Skating Rink:

Glide gracefully across the ice at the enchanting ice skating rink. Framed by the historic architecture of Bath, the rink becomes a picturesque setting for skaters of all ages. The soft glow of fairy lights illuminates the skating area, adding a touch of magic to this classic winter pastime.

Fire Pits and Cozy Seating Areas:

Warm up by crackling fire pits and cozy seating areas scattered throughout the market. These inviting spaces offer respite from the winter chill, allowing visitors to relax, enjoy a hot beverage, and savor the festive atmosphere in the company of friends and loved ones.

Twilight Illuminations:

As twilight descends, witness the market come alive with a mesmerizing display of twinkling lights and illuminations. The market square transforms into a captivating scene, with festive lights reflecting off the historic architecture, creating a magical ambiance that captures the essence of the holiday season.

Seasonal Workshops and Demonstrations:

Engage in seasonal workshops and demonstrations that invite visitors to unleash their creativity. From wreath-making to ornament crafting, these interactive experiences provide an opportunity for hands-on festive fun. Expert artisans guide participants through the art of creating personalized holiday decorations.

Candlelit Procession and Tree Lighting:

Join a candlelit procession through the market, culminating in the ceremonial lighting of the Christmas tree. The flickering candlelight creates a warm and communal atmosphere as visitors come together to witness the magic of the tree lighting, officially marking the beginning of the holiday season.

Farewell Fireworks Spectacle:

Bid farewell to the enchanting Christmas market with a dazzling fireworks spectacle that lights up the night sky. The colorful bursts of light create a breathtaking finale, leaving visitors with lasting memories of a magical winter wonderland experience in Bath.

"Christmas Market Magic in Bath" is not just a market; it's a symphony of festive delights, where the spirit of the season comes alive in every twinkling light, joyful carol, and heartwarming encounter. Visitors leave with hearts aglow, having experienced the epitome of holiday magic in the historic and charming city of Bath.

ICE SKATING IN GLOUCESTER QUAYS

Embark on a frosty escapade with the enchanting "Ice Skating in Gloucester Quays." Nestled in the heart of Gloucester, this winter wonderland experience invites visitors to lace up their skates and glide across a beautifully adorned ice rink, surrounded by festive lights and the historic charm of the Quays.

Grand Entrance to the Ice Skating Rink:

Begin your winter adventure with a grand entrance to the ice skating rink. Pass through festive archways adorned with twinkling lights, setting the stage for a magical experience. The ice rink, framed by historic architecture and festive decorations, becomes a picturesque scene that captures the spirit of the season.

Glistening Ice and Skating Pavilion:

Encounter the glistening expanse of the ice rink as you approach the skating pavilion. The ice, meticulously maintained for optimal gliding, beckons skaters of all ages to partake in the timeless winter activity. The pavilion, festooned with holiday decorations, exudes a cozy ambiance that complements the joyous atmosphere.

Skate Rentals and Warm Winter Attire:

Prepare for your ice skating adventure by renting skates at the pavilion. As you lace up your skates, embrace the opportunity to don warm winter attire, from cozy scarves to mittens. Skaters can choose from a variety of sizes and styles, ensuring a comfortable and stylish experience on the ice.

Festive Music and On-Ice Entertainment:

Glide across the ice to the backdrop of festive music that fills the air. The on-ice entertainment adds a delightful touch, with occasional performances or themed skate sessions that enhance the overall experience. Skaters can revel in the joyous atmosphere while enjoying the rhythmic sounds of the season.

Twinkling Lights and Festive Decorations:

Revel in the magical ambiance created by twinkling lights and festive decorations that adorn the perimeter of the ice rink. The combination of holiday lights reflecting off the ice creates a mesmerizing scene, transporting skaters into a winter wonderland right in the heart of Gloucester Quays.

Bavarian-Style Food and Hot Beverages:

Take a break from skating to indulge in Bavarian-style food stalls offering a delectable array of seasonal treats. From bratwurst to pretzels, these stalls provide a taste of winter delights. Warm up with hot beverages like mulled wine or hot cocoa, adding a touch of coziness to your ice skating experience.

Winter Market Stalls Alongside the Rink:

Explore winter market stalls conveniently located alongside the ice rink. These stalls showcase an array of festive goods, handmade crafts, and holiday gifts. Skaters can meander through the market, making it a one-stop destination for both winter activities and seasonal shopping.

Themed Skate Nights and Events:

Immerse yourself in the excitement of themed skate nights and special events. Whether it's a festive costume skate or a themed evening with music and lights, these events add an extra layer of fun to your ice skating experience. Check the schedule for announcements on upcoming themed nights.

Children's Skating Area and Ice Games:

Create magical memories for the little ones with a dedicated children's skating area. Here, young skaters can gain confidence on the ice in a safe and festive environment. Ice games and activities add an extra dimension of fun for children, ensuring that the ice skating experience is enjoyable for the whole family.

Evening Glow and Illuminated Surroundings:

Experience the enchantment of evening glow as the sun sets and the surroundings become illuminated. The combination of ambient lighting, festive decorations, and the glow of the ice creates a captivating atmosphere. Skaters can relish the unique beauty of evening ice skating in Gloucester Quays.

Ice Skating Lessons and Coaching (Optional):

For those looking to enhance their skating skills, consider optional ice skating lessons or coaching sessions. Qualified instructors provide personalized guidance, helping skaters of all levels improve their technique and confidence on the ice. Lessons can be tailored to individual or group needs.

Seasonal Ice Sculptures and Art Installations:

Admire seasonal ice sculptures and art installations strategically placed around the ice rink. These ephemeral creations add a touch of elegance to the winter wonderland, showcasing the artistry and craftsmanship of skilled ice sculptors. Skaters can enjoy these frozen masterpieces as they twirl on the ice.

Farewell Fireworks Spectacle (Select Nights):

Conclude your ice skating adventure with a spectacular farewell fireworks display on select nights. The fireworks spectacle lights up the night sky, providing a dazzling and memorable conclusion to your winter wonderland experience in Gloucester Quays.

"Ice Skating in Gloucester Quays" is not just a seasonal activity; it's a festive journey that combines the joy of skating with the magical ambiance of a winter wonderland. Whether you're a seasoned skater or lacing up your skates for the first time, this enchanting experience promises memorable moments and a true celebration of the season in the heart of Gloucester.

FESTIVE LIGHTS TOUR IN THE COTSWOLD VILLAGES

Embark on a magical journey through the heart of the Cotswolds with the "Festive Lights Tour in the Cotswold Villages." This enchanting experience invites visitors to explore the timeless charm of picturesque villages adorned with twinkling lights, creating a winter wonderland that captures the spirit of the season.

Cotswold Village Hubs:

Begin your festive adventure in one of the Cotswold village hubs, where the quaint charm and historic architecture set the stage for a magical evening. These village centers become the focal points for festive lights, creating a captivating atmosphere that draws visitors into the heart of the holiday spirit.

Twinkling Street Decorations:

Stroll through winding streets adorned with twinkling lights and tasteful decorations. Every corner unveils a new display of festive cheer, with illuminated garlands, sparkling ornaments, and creative lighting installations enhancing the character of each village. The timeless architecture serves as a picturesque backdrop to the enchanting scenes.

Shopfronts Aglow with Holiday Spirit:

Explore shopfronts aglow with holiday spirit, where local businesses join in the festive celebration. Each shop window becomes a canvas for creative and whimsical displays, showcasing holiday-themed decorations, winter scenes, and an array of seasonal merchandise. The warm glow emanating from the shops adds to the overall magic of the Cotswold villages.

Historic Landmarks Illuminated:

Marvel at historic landmarks illuminated in a soft, festive glow. From ancient churches to charming cottages, these landmarks take on a new level of enchantment under the twinkle of holiday lights. The play of light and shadow accentuates the architectural details, creating a captivating interplay between history and holiday festivity.

Decorated Village Squares:

Gather in decorated village squares where the heart of the festive celebrations unfolds. Christmas trees adorned with lights become the centerpiece, surrounded by cheerful decorations and sometimes a festive market. The village squares come alive with the sound of carolers, creating a communal space for locals and visitors alike to enjoy the season.

Warmth of Local Pubs and Cafés:

Seek refuge from the winter chill in the warmth of local pubs and cafés, where the glow of fireplace fires and twinkling lights welcomes visitors. Enjoy a cup of hot cocoa, mulled wine, or traditional seasonal treats as you soak in the cozy ambiance. These establishments become havens of comfort during the festive tour.

Themed Street Performances:

Encounter themed street performances that add a touch of entertainment to the festive atmosphere. From carol singers serenading passersby to street performers donning holiday-themed costumes, these spontaneous performances contribute to the joyful ambiance of the Cotswold villages during the winter season.

Hidden Courtyards and Alleyways:

Discover hidden courtyards and alleyways transformed into intimate corners of festive delight. These tucked-away spaces surprise visitors with charming light displays, creating intimate pockets of holiday magic. The play of light against ancient stone walls and cobbled paths adds a touch of enchantment to every step.

Guided Narratives and Local Stories:

Engage in guided narratives and local stories that bring the history and traditions of each village to life. Knowledgeable guides share anecdotes and tales of holiday celebrations in the Cotswolds, providing a deeper understanding of the cultural significance of the festive lights tour.

Candlelit Windows and Luminaries:

Experience the charm of candlelit windows and luminaries that line the streets. This timeless tradition imparts a warm and inviting glow to the village homes, creating a sense of unity and shared celebration. The flickering candlelight adds a nostalgic touch to the overall enchantment.

Village Churches Bathed in Light:

Stand in awe as village churches are bathed in a gentle wash of light. The architectural beauty of these historic churches is accentuated by carefully designed lighting, creating a serene and contemplative atmosphere. Attend a candlelit service or simply admire the illuminated facades from the village square.

Carriage Rides Through Illuminated Lanes (Optional):

Optionally, enhance your festive experience with carriage rides through illuminated lanes. A horse-drawn carriage becomes a cozy and nostalgic mode of transport, allowing visitors to leisurely explore the village streets while surrounded by the captivating glow of festive lights.

Firework Finale Over Village Skylines (Select Nights):

Conclude your Festive Lights Tour with a spectacular firework finale over the village skylines on select nights. The burst of colors against the dark winter sky creates a breathtaking spectacle, marking the culmination of a magical journey through the Cotswold villages.

The "Festive Lights Tour in the Cotswold Villages" is not just a visual feast; it's a celebration of community, tradition, and the timeless allure of the season. As you meander through the illuminated streets and experience the warmth of local hospitality, you'll carry with you the magic of a winter wonderland that defines the enchanting Cotswold villages during the holiday season.

FAMILY-FRIENDLY FUN

COTSWOLD FARM PARK ADVENTURE

Embark on a delightful family adventure at the Cotswold Farm Park, where the magic of the countryside comes alive. This family-friendly destination offers a perfect blend of hands-on experiences, animal encounters, and outdoor activities, creating lasting memories for visitors of all ages. Immerse yourself in the charm of rural life and discover the wonders that await at this Cotswold gem.

Meet the Cotswold Breeds:

Begin your adventure by meeting the charming Cotswold breeds that call the farm home. From fluffy lambs and curious piglets to friendly goats and majestic horses, the farm's diverse collection of animals provides a unique opportunity for children and adults alike to connect with rural life. Engage in feeding sessions and interactive experiences to get up close and personal with these adorable residents.

Hands-On Animal Encounters:

Delight in hands-on animal encounters that go beyond the typical petting zoo experience. Join interactive sessions where knowledgeable farm staff introduce you to the animals' habits, care, and unique characteristics. From grooming the ponies to handling chicks and ducklings, every encounter is a chance to learn and appreciate the diversity of farm life.

Explore Rare Breeds Conservation:

Immerse your family in the world of rare breed conservation at the farm. Learn about the importance of preserving traditional and endangered breeds that play a vital role in maintaining biodiversity. Engage with educational exhibits and discover how the farm contributes to safeguarding these unique animals, fostering an appreciation for sustainable farming practices.

Tractor Safari Adventure:

Climb aboard the Tractor Safari for an exciting adventure around the farm's picturesque landscape. Led by knowledgeable guides, this family-friendly safari offers a scenic journey through meadows and pastures. Learn about the farm's history, enjoy panoramic views of the Cotswold countryside, and spot various animals grazing in their natural habitats.

Outdoor Play Areas:

Unleash the energy of younger family members at the farm's outdoor play areas. From towering slides and climbing frames to imaginative play zones, these areas provide a safe and entertaining space for children to run, jump, and explore. The farm's commitment to family enjoyment ensures that children have ample opportunities for outdoor play and adventure.

Seasonal Activities and Events:

Experience the changing seasons with a calendar full of special activities and events. Whether it's lambing season, a harvest festival, or a festive Christmas celebration, the farm offers a variety of themed events throughout the year. Engage in seasonal crafts, participate in themed games, and create cherished family traditions during these special occasions.

Educational Farm Demonstrations:

Join engaging farm demonstrations that provide insights into daily farm life and activities. From sheep shearing and milking demonstrations to tractor driving lessons, these educational experiences offer a glimpse into the skills and traditions of farming. The interactive nature of the demonstrations ensures that learning becomes a fun and memorable experience for the whole family.

Wildlife Walks and Nature Trails:

Take leisurely walks along wildlife trails that wind through the farm's scenic surroundings. These nature trails provide opportunities to observe local flora and fauna, spot native bird species, and appreciate the natural beauty of the Cotswold landscape. Families can enjoy a peaceful escape while exploring the diverse ecosystems within and around the farm.

Farmyard Adventure Playground:

Let the little ones unleash their imagination at the Farmyard Adventure Playground. Designed with creativity and safety in mind, this playground features climbing structures, swings, and interactive play elements. Children can enjoy hours of outdoor fun, making new friends and burning off energy in a secure and welcoming environment.

Picnic Areas and Farm-Fresh Cuisine:

Relax and recharge at designated picnic areas where families can enjoy a leisurely meal surrounded by the picturesque Cotswold scenery. Alternatively, savor farm-fresh cuisine at the onsite cafe or restaurant, where locally sourced ingredients and seasonal delights take center stage. The farm's commitment to providing wholesome food adds an extra layer of enjoyment to your visit.

Animal Feeding Experiences:

Participate in animal feeding experiences that add an interactive dimension to your visit. From hand-feeding sheep and goats to offering treats to friendly donkeys, these experiences create lasting memories for children and adults alike. The joy of connecting with animals in a hands-on way enhances the overall farm adventure.

Pig Racing Spectacle:

Witness the excitement of pig racing, a hilarious and entertaining spectacle that captivates visitors of all ages. Cheer on your favorite piglet as they race towards the finish line, showcasing agility and speed. The pig racing events add a touch of whimsy to the farm experience and leave families laughing and clapping in delight.

Farm Shop and Souvenirs:

Conclude your adventure with a visit to the farm shop, where you can discover a range of farm-produced goods, including fresh produce, locally made treats, and unique souvenirs. Support local artisans and take home a piece of the Cotswold Farm Park experience, ensuring that the memories of your family-friendly adventure linger long after your visit.

The Cotswold Farm Park Adventure promises a wholesome and engaging experience for families, blending education, outdoor activities, and the joy of rural life. Whether you're feeding animals, enjoying outdoor play, or learning about conservation, this farm adventure creates a perfect balance of fun and discovery for every member of the family.

TREASURE HUNT IN PAINSWICK ROCOCO GARDEN

Embark on an enchanting family adventure at Painswick Rococo Garden, where the timeless charm of Rococo design meets the excitement of a treasure hunt. This family-friendly activity promises a delightful exploration of the garden's picturesque landscapes, hidden corners, and whimsical features. Get ready for a magical journey as you unravel clues, discover hidden treasures, and create lasting memories amidst the beauty of Painswick Rococo Garden.

Treasure Map Unveiling:

Begin your family treasure hunt adventure with the unveiling of a special treasure map. The map, adorned with Rococo-inspired illustrations, guides your family on a quest through the garden's winding pathways, enchanting groves, and blooming meadows. The anticipation builds as you study the map, eager to discover the hidden treasures that await.

Clue-Filled Garden Trails:

Set off on clue-filled garden trails that lead you to various points of interest within Painswick Rococo Garden. Each clue serves as a stepping stone in your quest, encouraging teamwork and problem-solving among family members. The trails take you on a journey through the garden's diverse landscapes, ensuring a rich and immersive experience.

Enchanting Rococo Features:

Marvel at the enchanting Rococo features scattered throughout the garden. From ornate follies and hidden archways to charming grottos and whimsical sculptures, these features become integral parts of your treasure hunt. As you follow the clues, discover the intricate details of Rococo design that add a touch of elegance to the garden's natural beauty.

Puzzles and Riddles:

Encounter puzzles and riddles strategically placed along the treasure hunt route. Engage your family's collective intellect as you decipher clues, solve puzzles, and unravel riddles that lead you closer to the hidden treasures. The interactive nature of these challenges adds an element of excitement and mental stimulation to the adventure.

Botanical Discoveries:

Immerse yourselves in the botanical wonders of Painswick Rococo Garden. The treasure hunt introduces you to rare and vibrant plant species, allowing you to appreciate the diversity of the garden's flora. Each botanical discovery becomes a piece of the puzzle, contributing to the overall tapestry of your family adventure.

Hidden Treasure Chests:

The culmination of your treasure hunt leads you to hidden treasure chests strategically placed throughout the garden. As you open each chest, the excitement peaks, revealing small surprises and mementos for your family to collect. These treasures serve as delightful keepsakes, commemorating the successful completion of your Rococo Garden adventure.

Scenic Rest Stops:

Take advantage of scenic rest stops along the treasure hunt route. Relax on inviting benches, enjoy panoramic views of the garden, and capture family photos against the backdrop of Rococo-inspired landscapes. These rest stops provide moments of respite and allow you to savor the tranquility of Painswick Rococo Garden.

Family Bonding Moments:

The treasure hunt becomes more than a quest for hidden treasures; it becomes a journey of family bonding. Collaborate, share laughter, and celebrate each discovery together. The shared sense of accomplishment enhances the familial connection, creating cherished memories that will be recounted for years to come.

Interactive Garden Activities:

Encounter interactive garden activities that complement the treasure hunt experience. Engage in nature-inspired games, explore sensory gardens, and participate in hands-on activities designed to captivate both children and adults. The garden's interactive elements add layers of enjoyment to your family-friendly adventure.

Rococo Tea Pavilion:

Conclude your treasure hunt with a visit to the Rococo Tea Pavilion. Nestled within the garden, this charming spot offers a delightful setting to relax and reflect on your adventure. Treat your family to a Rococo-inspired tea experience, complete with delectable treats and refreshing beverages, while surrounded by the garden's serene ambiance.

Treasure Hunt Certificates:

As a special memento of your family's Rococo Garden adventure, receive treasure hunt certificates upon completing the quest. Personalized with each family member's name, these certificates serve as tangible reminders of the joyous exploration and successful collaboration that defined your time in Painswick Rococo Garden.

The treasure hunt in Painswick Rococo Garden transforms a visit into a magical quest, blending the beauty of nature with the excitement of discovery. Whether unraveling clues, exploring Rococo features, or celebrating at the tea pavilion, this family-friendly adventure creates a perfect blend of enchantment and camaraderie within the timeless charm of the garden.

EXPLORE THE COTSWOLD MOTORING MUSEUM

Embark on a captivating family adventure as you step into the fascinating world of automotive history at the Cotswold Motoring Museum. Nestled in the heart of the Cotswolds, this family-friendly destination promises an immersive journey through decades of motoring evolution. From vintage cars and iconic motorcycles to interactive exhibits, the museum offers a delightful experience for visitors of all ages.

Entrance into Motoring History:

Begin your journey by stepping through the doors of the Cotswold Motoring Museum. The entrance sets the tone for a captivating exploration, with vintage automobiles and classic motorcycles on display, creating an immediate sense of nostalgia and excitement.

Vintage Car Collection:

Marvel at the impressive collection of vintage cars that span the timeline of automotive history. From elegant pre-war models to iconic post-war classics, each car tells a story of design, engineering, and the evolution of motoring culture. The carefully curated exhibit showcases the beauty and craftsmanship of automobiles from different eras.

Iconic Motorcycles Display:

Immerse yourself in the world of two-wheel wonders as you explore the display of iconic motorcycles. From sleek and streamlined designs to rugged off-road models, the motorcycle exhibit pays homage to the diverse and dynamic history of these two-wheeled machines. Learn about the evolution of motorcycle technology and design through the decades.

Interactive Exhibits for All Ages:

Engage in interactive exhibits designed to captivate visitors of all ages. From hands-on displays that explain the inner workings of engines to interactive quizzes and games, the museum ensures that learning about motoring history is an enjoyable and participatory experience for the entire family.

Child-Friendly Activities:

Create lasting memories with child-friendly activities scattered throughout the museum. Younger visitors can enjoy coloring stations, interactive touchscreens, and educational games tailored to their age group. The child-friendly approach adds an element of fun and discovery to the museum visit, making it an enjoyable experience for the whole family.

Motoring Memorabilia and Artifacts:

Explore a treasure trove of motoring memorabilia and artifacts that provide insight into the bygone era of motoring. From vintage advertisements and fuel pumps to motoring accessories and period clothing, these displays offer a glimpse into the culture and lifestyle surrounding early motoring.

Historic Garages and Workshops:

Wander through recreated historic garages and workshops that transport you back in time. Admire the tools, equipment, and signage that adorned these early motoring establishments. The attention to detail in these exhibits allows you to visualize the craftsmanship and dedication of automotive enthusiasts and mechanics from the past.

Motoring Stories and Narratives:

Immerse yourself in motoring stories and narratives that bring the exhibits to life. Audio guides and informative placards provide context and anecdotes, allowing visitors to connect with the human stories behind each vehicle. Gain a deeper understanding of the personal journeys and adventures associated with the showcased cars and motorcycles.

Vintage Fuel Station Display:

Transport yourself to a bygone era with a display of a vintage fuel station. Complete with period pumps, signage, and accessories, this exhibit captures the essence of early motoring refueling stations. The nostalgic ambiance adds a touch of authenticity to the museum, enhancing the overall experience.

Period-Perfect Street Scenes:

Stroll through meticulously recreated period-perfect street scenes that evoke the charm of different motoring eras. From cobbled streets to quaint village settings, these exhibits provide a backdrop for the displayed vehicles, allowing you to imagine the sights and sounds of motoring in days gone by.

Motoring Evolution Timeline:

Follow the motoring evolution timeline that chronicles the major milestones and innovations in automotive history. From the invention of the first automobiles to breakthroughs in design and technology, the timeline offers a comprehensive overview, making the museum visit an educational and enriching experience for visitors of all ages.

Museum Shop and Souvenirs:

Conclude your exploration with a visit to the museum shop, where you can find motoring-themed souvenirs, model cars, and vintage-inspired merchandise. Whether you're a car enthusiast or looking for a memento of your visit, the shop offers a delightful array of items to commemorate your time at the Cotswold Motoring Museum.

The Cotswold Motoring Museum seamlessly blends education and entertainment, offering a family-friendly experience that appeals to motoring enthusiasts and curious minds alike. Whether you're marveling at vintage cars, engaging in interactive exhibits, or stepping into recreated historic scenes, the museum invites you to embark on a journey through the rich tapestry of automotive history in the heart of the Cotswolds.

SHOPPING AND MARKETS

BROWSE THE COTSWOLD FARMERS' MARKETS

Immerse yourself in the vibrant tapestry of local flavors, artisanal crafts, and community spirit as you explore the Cotswold Farmers' Markets. These markets, scattered across picturesque towns and villages, offer a sensory-rich experience where the region's agricultural bounty and artisanal craftsmanship take center stage.

Market Square Atmosphere:

Step into the lively ambiance of the Cotswold Farmers' Markets, where market squares come alive with the hustle and bustle of vendors, locals, and visitors. The charming setting, often surrounded by historic buildings, sets the stage for a delightful shopping experience.

Fresh Produce Stalls:

Begin your exploration by perusing the fresh produce stalls adorned with an array of seasonal fruits, vegetables, and herbs. From plump berries to heirloom tomatoes, the stalls showcase the diversity and quality of locally grown produce.

Artisanal Baked Goods:

Indulge your senses with the aroma of freshly baked goods emanating from artisanal bakeries. Crusty loaves, delicate pastries, and savory treats tempt passersby, inviting you to savor the craftsmanship of local bakers.

Local Dairy Delights:

Discover a selection of local cheeses, from creamy Brie to crumbly cheddars, presented by passionate cheesemongers. Engage in tastings and learn about the artisanal techniques that contribute to the unique flavors of Cotswold cheeses.

Farm-Fresh Meats and Poultry:

Peruse the stalls of local farmers offering farm-fresh meats and poultry. The variety ranges from succulent cuts of beef and lamb to free-range poultry, reflecting the commitment to sustainable and ethical farming practices.

Floral and Garden Stalls:

Delight in the vibrant colors and fragrances of floral and garden stalls. From seasonal blooms to potted herbs, these stalls add a touch of nature to the market, providing an opportunity to bring a bit of the Cotswold countryside home.

Handcrafted Artisanal Products:

Explore stalls showcasing handcrafted artisanal products, including pottery, textiles, and home decor. Local artisans bring their skills to the market, offering one-of-a-kind treasures that capture the essence of Cotswold craftsmanship.

Gourmet Delicacies:

Indulge in gourmet delights, from locally produced jams and chutneys to infused oils and specialty condiments. The market provides a curated selection of gastronomic treasures that reflect the culinary richness of the Cotswolds.

Culinary Demonstrations:

Immerse yourself in culinary demonstrations where local chefs showcase their expertise. Learn cooking tips, recipe ideas, and gain insights into how to make the most of the fresh, seasonal ingredients available at the market.

Live Music and Entertainment:

Enjoy the lively atmosphere enhanced by live music and street performers. The musical backdrop and entertainment contribute to the festive spirit of the Cotswold Farmers' Markets, creating a sense of community celebration.

Street Food and Ready-to-Eat Delights:

Treat your taste buds to a diverse array of street food offerings and ready-to-eat delights. From gourmet sandwiches to international cuisines, the market provides a culinary journey for those seeking a quick and flavorful bite.

Children's Activities and Petting Zoos:

Engage younger visitors with children's activities and petting zoos. The family-friendly atmosphere ensures that the Cotswold Farmers' Markets cater to all ages, fostering a sense of community and shared enjoyment.

Seasonal Festivals and Themes:

Attend special market events tied to seasonal festivals or themes. These occasions bring an added layer of festivity, with decorations, themed offerings, and community celebrations that enhance the overall market experience.

Community Engagement:

Connect with local farmers, artisans, and producers who are passionate about their craft. Engage in conversations about the products, learn about sustainable practices, and gain insights into the stories behind the items available at the market.

Browsing the Cotswold Farmers' Markets is not just a shopping excursion; it's a holistic experience that celebrates the region's agricultural heritage, artisanal craftsmanship, and sense of community. Each stall, each interaction, and each purchase contribute to a narrative of local pride and a shared commitment to preserving the distinctive character of the Cotswolds.

ANTIQUE HUNTING IN STOW-ON-THE-WOLD

Embark on a treasure hunt through the historic streets of Stow-on-the-Wold, where the past comes to life in the myriad antique shops that line the charming market town. Antique hunting in Stow-on-the-Wold is a captivating journey filled with timeless pieces, unique finds, and the enchanting stories that accompany each carefully curated item.

Cobbled Streets and Market Square:

Begin your adventure on the cobbled streets of Stow-on-the-Wold, where every step echoes with the town's rich history. The market square, surrounded by honey-colored stone buildings, sets the scene for an antique exploration that transports you to bygone eras.

Antique Shopfronts and Window Displays:

As you approach the antique shops, be captivated by the allure of their shopfronts. Intricate window displays beckon, offering glimpses into the world of vintage treasures and antique wonders that lie within.

Variety of Antique Shops:

Stow-on-the-Wold boasts a diverse array of antique shops, each with its own character and specialization. From quaint boutiques to expansive emporiums, you'll find a treasure trove of antique furniture, vintage curiosities, and collectibles awaiting your discovery.

Timeless Furniture Finds:

Explore shops dedicated to antique furniture, where each piece tells a tale of craftsmanship and enduring design. From elegant Victorian dressers to rustic farmhouse tables, the selection caters to a range of tastes and styles.

Vintage Curios and Oddities:

Uncover shops specializing in vintage curiosities and oddities. Delve into a world of quirky artifacts, nostalgic trinkets, and eccentric pieces that add character to your home and evoke a sense of whimsical nostalgia.

Art and Decor Galleries:

Immerse yourself in galleries that showcase antique art and decor. Admire ornate frames, timeless paintings, and decorative accents that capture the essence of different artistic movements and periods.

Collectibles and Memorabilia:

Seek out shops dedicated to collectibles and memorabilia. From vintage postcards to rare coins, these troves offer collectors and history enthusiasts a chance to unearth hidden gems and relics of the past.

Antique Books and Manuscripts:

Discover hidden corners dedicated to antique books and manuscripts. Lose yourself in the scent of aged pages as you peruse shelves lined with leather-bound volumes, first editions, and handwritten manuscripts that carry the weight of history.

Silverware and Fine China:

Indulge in the elegance of antique silverware and fine china. Shops specializing in these treasures present a dazzling array of teacups, silver spoons, and delicate plates that exude timeless sophistication.

Knowledgeable Shopkeepers:

Engage with knowledgeable shopkeepers who are passionate about the history and provenance of their antique offerings. Their insights, stories, and expertise add a layer of depth to your antique hunting experience.

Period Clothing and Accessories:

Step into shops dedicated to period clothing and accessories. Explore racks adorned with vintage dresses, hats, and accessories that transport you to a different era, allowing you to embrace the timeless fashion of days gone by.

Antique Restoration Workshops:

Encounter antique restoration workshops where skilled artisans breathe new life into aged pieces. Witness the meticulous craftsmanship involved in preserving the authenticity and charm of each item, ensuring it stands the test of time.

Charming Tea Rooms and Cafés:

Take a leisurely break in charming tea rooms and cafés that dot the antique-hunting route. Reflect on your discoveries over a cup of tea or coffee, surrounded by the timeless ambiance of Stow-on-the-Wold.

Scenic Views and Hidden Gems:

As you explore the town, appreciate scenic views of the surrounding Cotswold countryside. Stumble upon hidden gems, from tucked-away bookshops to quaint corners with antique stalls, adding an element of serendipity to your antique hunting adventure.

Antique hunting in Stow-on-the-Wold is not merely a shopping experience; it's a journey through time, guided by the stories of each artifact and the passion of those who preserve the town's antique legacy. Every find becomes a cherished piece of history, carrying with it the charm and allure of Stow-on-the-Wold's rich heritage.

SHOP FOR LOCAL CRAFTS IN CHIPPING CAMPDEN

Embark on a delightful shopping excursion in the idyllic town of Chipping Campden, where the streets are lined with charming shops offering an array of locally crafted treasures. From handmade textiles to bespoke ceramics, the experience of shopping for local crafts in Chipping Campden is a journey into the heart of artisanal excellence and Cotswold craftsmanship.

Quaint Market Town Atmosphere:

Begin your exploration in the heart of Chipping Campden, where the quaint market town atmosphere creates a welcoming backdrop for your shopping adventure. Cobblestone streets and historic buildings set the scene for an enchanting experience.

Artisan Boutiques and Studios:

Wander through artisan boutiques and studios that showcase the talents of local craftspeople. Each establishment offers a curated selection of handcrafted goods, ensuring a diverse range of items reflecting the skill and creativity of the Cotswold artisans.

Handwoven Textiles and Fabrics:

Explore shops specializing in handwoven textiles and fabrics. From cozy blankets to intricately woven scarves, these pieces showcase the artistry of local weavers. Feel the quality of each textile, rich in both tradition and contemporary flair.

Bespoke Ceramics and Pottery:

Immerse yourself in the world of bespoke ceramics and pottery. Admire shelves adorned with one-of-a-kind pieces, from intricately painted plates to elegantly glazed vases. The craftsmanship of local potters transforms functional items into works of art.

Jewelry Workshops and Boutiques:

Indulge in jewelry workshops and boutiques that offer handmade treasures. From delicate silver earrings to statement necklaces, these shops provide a haven for those seeking unique and locally crafted adornments.

Woodcraft and Artisan Furniture:

Appreciate the art of woodcraft and artisan furniture. Explore workshops and showrooms where skilled craftsmen transform wood into bespoke pieces, from intricately carved furniture to hand-turned bowls that celebrate the natural beauty of timber.

Stained Glass Studios:

Encounter stained glass studios that illuminate Chipping Campden with colorful creations. Browse through panels, ornaments, and bespoke stained glass pieces that capture the play of light and color, adding a touch of artistry to your surroundings.

Leatherwork and Bespoke Accessories:

Delve into the world of leatherwork and bespoke accessories. Discover shops that offer hand-stitched leather goods, from finely crafted wallets to custom-made belts. The aroma of quality leather fills the air, inviting you to appreciate the tactile beauty of each piece.

Art Galleries and Local Paintings:

Explore art galleries featuring local paintings and artworks. The galleries showcase the talent of Cotswold artists, capturing the essence of the region's landscapes and heritage in brushstrokes that evoke a sense of place.

Candle and Soap Ateliers:

Immerse yourself in candle and soap ateliers that bring aromatic delights to Chipping Campden. Hand-poured candles and artisanal soaps showcase a commitment to quality ingredients and craftsmanship, offering sensory pleasures for your home.

Glassblowing Workshops:

Witness the art of glassblowing in workshops that showcase the mesmerizing process of shaping molten glass into exquisite forms.

From delicate ornaments to vibrant glassware, each piece is a testament to the skill of local glass artisans.

Textile Printing Studios:

Engage with textile printing studios where fabrics come to life with bespoke designs. Browse through printed cushions, linens, and clothing items that showcase the creativity and attention to detail of local textile artisans.

Cozy Art Cafés and Tea Rooms:

Take a break in cozy art cafés and tea rooms scattered throughout Chipping Campden. Reflect on your finds over a cup of tea or coffee, surrounded by the ambiance of these charming establishments that often double as showcases for local artwork.

Hidden Courtyards and Craft Markets:

Discover hidden courtyards and craft markets that unveil additional gems. These spaces, tucked away from the main streets, often host pop-up markets and events, providing an opportunity to encounter even more local crafts and artisanal delights.

Shopping for local crafts in Chipping Campden is a sensory journey that connects you with the artistic soul of the Cotswolds. Each handmade piece tells a story of tradition, creativity, and the enduring spirit of craftsmanship that defines this charming market town.

LEARN TRADITIONAL CRAFTS

COTSWOLD DRY STONE WALLING WORKSHOP

Embark on a hands-on journey into the age-old craft of dry stone walling with the "Cotswold Dry Stone Walling Workshop." Set against the backdrop of the picturesque Cotswold countryside, this immersive experience invites participants to learn the intricacies of constructing durable and beautiful dry stone walls, a traditional craft deeply rooted in the region's heritage.

Introduction to Dry Stone Walling:

Begin the workshop with an introduction to the rich history and cultural significance of dry stone walling in the Cotswolds. Participants gain insights into how this traditional craft has shaped the landscape, served practical purposes, and become an iconic feature of the region's rural charm.

Selection of Stone:

Engage in the hands-on process of selecting suitable stones for dry stone wall construction. Participants learn to discern the characteristics of different stones, considering factors such as size, shape, and durability. This initial step sets the foundation for creating structurally sound and aesthetically pleasing walls.

Tools of the Trade:

Familiarize yourself with the tools used in dry stone walling. From hammers and chisels to line levels and pegs, participants gain hands-on experience with the essential tools required for precision in crafting dry stone walls. Instructors provide guidance on tool usage, safety protocols, and maintaining craftsmanship standards.

Foundation and Footing Techniques:

Explore the crucial techniques involved in laying a strong foundation and creating a stable footing for the dry stone wall. Instructors guide participants through the process of leveling the ground, setting the initial stones, and establishing a solid base that ensures the longevity and integrity of the structure.

Building Techniques and Styles:

Delve into the diverse building techniques and styles employed in dry stone walling. Participants learn about single and double-faced walls, hearting and through stones, and the art of creating a wall that seamlessly blends with the natural landscape. Instructors provide demonstrations and hands-on practice to hone these foundational skills.

Interlocking Stones and Structural Integrity:

Master the art of interlocking stones to enhance the structural integrity of the dry stone wall. Participants discover how to strategically place stones, ensuring stability and durability while maintaining a visually pleasing pattern. This session emphasizes the craftsmanship required to create walls that stand the test of time.

Creativity in Design:

Encourage creativity in design as participants progress to constructing sections of the dry stone wall. Instructors guide individuals in experimenting with patterns, textures, and variations in stone placement. This hands-on approach allows participants to infuse their personality into the craftsmanship while adhering to the fundamental principles of dry stone walling.

Building Height and Tapering:

Explore the considerations for building height and tapering in dry stone walls. Participants gain an understanding of how to gradually taper the structure to maintain stability and prevent collapse. Instructors provide insights into achieving a harmonious balance between the height of the wall and its overall aesthetic appeal.

Repair and Maintenance Techniques:

Learn essential repair and maintenance techniques to ensure the longevity of dry stone walls. Participants acquire skills in identifying and addressing issues such as displaced stones, erosion, and structural weaknesses. Instructors share insights into the cyclical nature of dry stone wall maintenance and the importance of ongoing care.

Team Collaboration and Wall Completion:

Collaborate with fellow participants to collectively build a section of the dry stone wall. This collaborative effort fosters teamwork, communication, and a shared sense of accomplishment as the wall takes shape. Instructors provide guidance and support to ensure a cohesive and well-constructed final product.

Landscaping Integration:

Explore techniques for integrating dry stone walls seamlessly into the surrounding landscape. Participants learn how to adapt their craftsmanship to the natural contours of the land, creating walls that not only serve practical purposes but also enhance the scenic beauty of the Cotswold countryside.

Group Reflection and Showcase:

Conclude the workshop with a group reflection and showcase session. Participants share their experiences, challenges overcome, and the unique characteristics of the sections they contributed to the dry stone wall. Instructors provide feedback and celebrate the collective achievement of creating a lasting testament to traditional craftsmanship.

Certificate of Completion and Resources:

Receive a certificate of completion recognizing your participation in the Cotswold Dry Stone Walling Workshop. Instructors provide additional resources, including recommended reading materials, online tutorials, and local contacts for those eager to continue exploring and mastering the craft of dry stone walling.

The Cotswold Dry Stone Walling Workshop not only imparts practical skills in a traditional craft but also fosters a deeper connection to the cultural heritage and natural beauty of the Cotswolds. Through hands-on learning, participants contribute to the preservation of this timeless craft, leaving a lasting mark on the landscape they've helped shape.

WILLOW WEAVING IN STROUD

Embark on a creative and hands-on journey into the age-old art of willow weaving with the "Willow Weaving in Stroud" workshop. Nestled in the heart of the Cotswolds, this immersive experience invites participants to connect with nature, explore their artistic side, and craft beautiful and functional items using the versatile and sustainable material of willow.

Introduction to Willow Weaving:

Begin the workshop with a warm welcome and an introduction to the fascinating world of willow weaving. Participants gain insights into the historical roots of this traditional craft, its cultural significance, and the sustainable nature of willow as a versatile material.

Varieties of Willow and Material Selection:

Explore the varieties of willow available and learn the art of selecting the right material for different weaving projects. Instructors guide participants through the characteristics of various willow types, emphasizing the importance of flexibility, color, and thickness for specific creations.

Basic Weaving Techniques:

Dive into basic weaving techniques, starting with fundamental patterns and structures. Participants receive hands-on instruction on how to handle and manipulate willow strands, creating a solid foundation for more intricate projects. Instructors provide demonstrations and one-on-one guidance to ensure a grasp of essential weaving skills.

Creating a Willow Base:

Progress to creating a willow base, the foundation for many weaving projects. Participants learn to shape and form the willow into a sturdy structure, understanding the importance of tension, spacing, and symmetry. This step lays the groundwork for a variety of items, from baskets to decorative pieces.

Crafting a Simple Basket:

Take the first steps in basketry by crafting a simple yet elegant willow basket. Instructors provide a step-by-step guide, assisting participants in weaving the sides, adding handles, and finishing with a tailored rim. The focus is on achieving a harmonious balance between functionality and aesthetics.

Advanced Weaving Patterns:

Explore advanced weaving patterns and techniques as participants gain confidence in their skills. Instructors introduce more intricate patterns, allowing for creative expression and personalized touches. Participants have the opportunity to experiment with different weaves, colors, and textures to enhance their creations.

Willow Sculptures and Decorative Forms:

Expand beyond functional items to explore the art of creating willow sculptures and decorative forms. Participants discover the potential of willow as a sculptural medium, shaping it into animals, abstract forms, or intricate patterns. Instructors provide inspiration and guidance for those eager to push the boundaries of traditional weaving.

Weaving Garden Structures:

Learn how to weave practical and aesthetically pleasing garden structures using willow. Participants delve into projects such as trellises, plant supports, or even living willow structures that grow and evolve over time. Instructors share insights into incorporating willow weaving into garden design.

Natural Dyes and Finishing Touches:

Explore the use of natural dyes to add color and character to woven creations. Participants learn how to create dyes from plant materials, infusing their projects with vibrant hues. Instructors guide the application of dyes and provide tips for finishing touches to enhance the overall appearance.

Sustainable Practices and Harvesting Tips:

Gain an understanding of sustainable practices in willow weaving and learn harvesting tips to ensure the responsible and eco-friendly use of willow. Instructors discuss the seasonal considerations for harvesting, promoting a respectful and mindful approach to working with this renewable resource.

Group Collaboration and Showcase:

Collaborate with fellow participants on a group project that showcases the collective creativity of the workshop. Whether it's a large woven installation or a community art piece, the group collaboration fosters teamwork and a sense of shared accomplishment. Participants celebrate their collective creation in a showcase session.

Individual Project and Personal Reflection:

Dedicate time to work on individual projects, allowing participants to express their unique artistic vision. Instructors offer personalized guidance as participants focus on a specific weaving project that aligns with their interests. The workshop provides an opportunity for personal reflection and creative exploration.

Gallery Walk and Artisan Market:

Conclude the workshop with a gallery walk and visit to an artisan market showcasing willow creations. Participants have the chance to admire each other's work, exchange ideas, and explore additional handmade willow items crafted by local artisans. The market provides a platform to support the vibrant community of willow weavers.

Certificate of Completion and Resource Guide:

Receive a certificate of completion to commemorate your participation in the Willow Weaving in Stroud workshop. Instructors provide a resource guide, including recommended reading materials, online tutorials, and local contacts for further exploration of willow weaving and related crafts.

The Willow Weaving in Stroud workshop not only imparts practical skills but also fosters a deep appreciation for nature, sustainable practices, and the artistic possibilities of working with willow. Participants leave with both beautiful creations and the knowledge to continue their journey into the time-honored craft of willow weaving.

POTTERY CLASS IN CHIPPING CAMPDEN

Immerse yourself in the timeless art of pottery with the "Pottery Class in Chipping Campden." Nestled in the heart of the Cotswolds, this hands-on workshop offers a unique opportunity to explore the tactile world of clay, from its raw form to beautifully crafted ceramic creations.

Introduction to Pottery:

Begin your pottery journey with a warm welcome and an introduction to the rich history and significance of pottery. Participants gain insights into the cultural heritage of pottery, the diverse styles within the craft, and its enduring appeal as a form of artistic expression.

Exploration of Clay Types:

Dive into the world of clay as you explore different types and varieties. Instructors guide participants through the characteristics of clay, emphasizing its unique properties and suitability for various pottery techniques. Gain an understanding of how clay composition impacts the final outcome of your creations.

Basic Hand-Building Techniques:

Learn fundamental hand-building techniques, such as coiling, pinching, and slab construction. Participants engage in hands-on exercises to shape clay into basic forms, laying the groundwork for more intricate projects. Instructors provide step-by-step guidance, ensuring a solid grasp of essential hand-building skills.

Wheel Throwing Basics:

Transition to the potter's wheel for an introduction to wheel throwing. Participants experience the mesmerizing process of centering clay on the wheel, forming vessels, and bringing their unique artistic vision to life. Instructors offer personalized guidance to individuals as they navigate the wheel throwing process.

Creating Functional Pieces:

Explore the creation of functional pottery pieces such as mugs, bowls, and plates. Participants delve into the nuances of form, proportion, and functionality, guided by instructors who share insights into designing pieces that are both aesthetically pleasing and practical for everyday use.

Surface Decoration Techniques:

Embark on the artistic journey of surface decoration. Participants learn techniques such as carving, slip trailing, and underglaze application to add texture, patterns, and visual interest to their pottery. Instructors provide demonstrations and encourage creative experimentation with various decorating methods.

Glazing and Firing Process:

Gain an understanding of the glazing process and the transformative effects it has on pottery. Instructors guide participants through glaze selection, application methods, and the science behind the firing process. Witness the magic of kiln firing as your creations undergo the final transformation into vibrant and durable pieces of art.

Raku Firing Experience (Optional):

Optionally, participate in a Raku firing experience to add an extra layer of excitement to your pottery journey. Raku firing, known for its unpredictable and dynamic results, involves removing red-hot pieces from the kiln and placing them in combustible materials. Witness the unique surface effects that emerge during this exhilarating process.

Individual Project and Personal Expression:

Dedicate time to work on an individual project, allowing participants to express their unique artistic voice. Instructors provide one-on-one support as individuals focus on a specific pottery piece that aligns with their interests and creative vision. The workshop encourages personal expression and exploration.

Group Critique and Feedback:

Engage in a group critique session where participants have the opportunity to share their creations, insights, and challenges. Instructors provide constructive feedback, fostering a supportive and collaborative environment. The group critique enhances the learning experience and encourages a sense of community among participants.

Gallery Exhibition and Artisan Market:

Conclude the workshop with a gallery exhibition and visit to an artisan market showcasing the diverse pottery creations. Participants showcase their work, exchange ideas, and explore additional handmade pottery items crafted by local artisans. The market provides a platform to support the vibrant community of pottery enthusiasts.

Certificate of Completion and Resource Guide:

Receive a certificate of completion to commemorate your participation in the Pottery Class in Chipping Campden. Instructors provide a resource guide, including recommended reading materials, online tutorials, and local contacts for those eager to continue exploring the art of pottery.

The Pottery Class in Chipping Campden not only imparts practical skills but also nurtures a deep appreciation for the artistry, craftsmanship, and creative possibilities inherent in pottery. Participants leave with both functional and decorative pottery pieces, as well as the inspiration to continue their artistic exploration in the world of ceramics.

ADMIRE STAINED GLASS

GLOUCESTER CATHEDRAL STAINED GLASS TOUR

Embark on a captivating journey through the sublime artistry of stained glass with the Gloucester Cathedral Stained Glass Tour. This immersive experience invites visitors to explore the rich history, intricate craftsmanship, and breathtaking beauty of the stained glass windows adorning the magnificent Gloucester Cathedral. As you traverse the hallowed halls, each window unveils a story, a testament to the convergence of art, spirituality, and architectural splendor.

Historical Context:

Begin your stained glass tour with an introduction to the historical context of Gloucester Cathedral. Gain insights into the architectural significance of the cathedral and its role in preserving the medieval art of stained glass. The narrative sets the stage for a profound appreciation of the artistic treasures that await within.

Medieval Masterpieces:

Marvel at the medieval masterpieces that grace the cathedral's windows. Each panel is a work of art, meticulously crafted by skilled artisans who, over the centuries, have contributed to the cathedral's impressive collection. Admire the vibrant colors, intricate details, and storytelling elements that characterize these timeless stained glass creations.

Iconic Stained Glass Windows:

Encounter iconic stained glass windows that serve as focal points within the cathedral. From the majestic Great East Window to the awe-inspiring Lady Chapel windows, each installation boasts unique narratives and artistic styles. Discover the symbolism embedded in the glass, conveying biblical stories, saints' lives, and historical events with profound visual impact.

The Great East Window:

Delve into the splendor of the Great East Window, a masterpiece of medieval stained glass artistry. This monumental window depicts the biblical narrative from Genesis to Revelation, unfolding the entire story of salvation. Stand in awe of the sheer scale, intricate details, and theological depth encapsulated in this magnum opus of stained glass craftsmanship.

Lady Chapel Windows:

Immerse yourself in the tranquility of the Lady Chapel, surrounded by its exquisite stained glass windows. The soft hues and delicate details create an ambiance of serenity, enhancing the spiritual experience. Explore themes of devotion, grace, and the divine feminine as depicted in these carefully curated windows.

Tombs and Stained Glass Combinations:

Appreciate the synergy between tombs and stained glass as you encounter sections where ornate tombs are complemented by intricate stained glass installations. The interplay of light and color adds a poignant dimension to the stories of individuals memorialized in the cathedral, creating a harmonious blend of artistic expression and historical commemoration.

The Creation Window:

Stand before the awe-inspiring Creation Window, a visual symphony depicting the Genesis narrative. Admire the meticulous detailing of flora, fauna, and human figures as the window unfolds the story of the world's creation. The play of light through this extraordinary piece transforms the cathedral space into a canvas of divine imagination.

Craftsmanship Revealed:

Gain a deeper understanding of stained glass craftsmanship through insights into the techniques employed by medieval artisans. Learn about the use of colored glass, lead caming, and the art of painting on glass. The tour provides a rare glimpse into the skillful hands and creative minds that brought these masterpieces to life.

Symbolism and Spiritual Significance:

Explore the symbolism and spiritual significance embedded in each pane of glass. From saints and biblical scenes to heraldic motifs, decipher the layers of meaning woven into the tapestry of stained glass art. The tour guides you in unraveling the language of symbols, fostering a deeper connection to the spiritual messages conveyed.

Educational Narratives:

Engage with educational narratives woven into the tour, providing enriching context to the stories depicted in the stained glass windows. Whether exploring the lives of saints, biblical events, or historical milestones, the educational component enhances your appreciation for the artistic and cultural legacy preserved within Gloucester Cathedral.

Interactive Elements:

Encounter interactive elements within the tour, allowing visitors to engage with the stained glass experience on a deeper level. Touchscreen displays, augmented reality features, or multimedia presentations may complement traditional storytelling, providing a multi-sensory exploration of the stained glass artistry.

Conservation Efforts:

Learn about the ongoing conservation efforts dedicated to preserving these invaluable treasures. Gain insight into the challenges of maintaining medieval stained glass and the measures taken to ensure the longevity of these artistic marvels. Appreciate the dedication to safeguarding cultural heritage for future generations.

Visitor Engagement Opportunities:

Participate in visitor engagement opportunities, such as workshops or guided discussions, allowing you to share impressions, ask questions, and delve into the intricacies of stained glass art. These interactive sessions provide a platform for a deeper connection with both the art and fellow visitors.

Reflective Spaces:

Take advantage of reflective spaces within the cathedral, where you can pause and absorb the beauty of the stained glass in a contemplative atmosphere. These designated areas invite moments of quiet introspection, allowing you to connect with the spirituality and artistic brilliance encapsulated in the windows.

The Gloucester Cathedral Stained Glass Tour is a transcendent exploration of artistic mastery, spiritual resonance, and historical significance. As you navigate the radiant tapestry of stained glass, you not only witness the craftsmanship of bygone eras but also embark on a soul-stirring journey through narratives that have stood the test of time within the sacred walls of Gloucester Cathedral.

ST. EDWARD'S CHURCH STAINED GLASS EXHIBITION

Step into a realm of ethereal beauty and spiritual illumination with the St. Edward's Church Stained Glass Exhibition. Nestled within the sacred confines of St. Edward's Church, this enchanting display of stained glass artistry transcends time, offering visitors a mesmerizing journey through intricate designs, vibrant colors, and profound narratives. Immerse yourself in the divine radiance of these magnificent windows as they weave tales of faith, history, and artistic brilliance.

Introduction to St. Edward's Church:

Begin your exploration with an introduction to the historical and spiritual significance of St. Edward's Church. Learn about the architectural elements that provide the perfect backdrop for the stained glass exhibition. The church's serene ambiance sets the stage for a contemplative and immersive experience.

Medieval Craftsmanship Unveiled:

Marvel at the craftsmanship of medieval artisans as you encounter the stained glass windows that adorn St. Edward's Church. Each panel is a testament to the skill and dedication of those who crafted these masterpieces, showcasing the precision of leaded glasswork, vibrant pigments, and delicate details that define the medieval stained glass tradition.

Architectural Integration:

Appreciate how the stained glass seamlessly integrates with the church's architecture. The windows serve not only as decorative elements but also as integral components of the sacred space, casting a kaleidoscope of colors that dance across the stone walls. The harmonious fusion of architecture and stained glass enhances the overall visual and spiritual experience.

Biblical Narratives Illuminated:

Engage with the biblical narratives illuminated through the stained glass windows. Each panel tells a story, depicting scenes from the Old and New Testaments with artistic flair and interpretive depth. Witness the visual storytelling unfold as you traverse the church, with windows that narrate the lives of saints, biblical events, and sacred traditions.

The Play of Light and Color:

Experience the enchanting play of light and color as sunlight filters through the stained glass, creating a mesmerizing interplay of hues that bathes the interior in a warm and divine glow. The dynamic relationship between light and glass amplifies the emotional impact of the narratives, evoking a sense of wonder and reverence.

Symbolism in Glass:

Explore the symbolism embedded in the stained glass panels. From symbolic colors to intricate patterns and motifs, each element carries profound meaning. The exhibition provides insights into the language of symbolism, allowing visitors to decipher the hidden messages and theological significance woven into the fabric of each window.

Unique Styles and Artistic Expressions:

Encounter a diverse array of styles and artistic expressions within the stained glass exhibition. From the elegant lines of Gothic tracery to the rich colors of Renaissance-inspired designs, the windows showcase the evolution of stained glass art over the centuries. Appreciate the unique contributions of different periods and artistic movements.

Memorial Windows and Commemorative Art:

Pay homage to memorial windows and commemorative art that celebrate the lives of individuals and families associated with the church. These windows serve as poignant tributes, blending artistic expression with personal remembrance. Discover the stories behind each memorial window and the lives they honor.

Choir and Chancel Windows:

Admire the beauty of stained glass in the choir and chancel areas, where specially designed windows enhance the worship experience. These windows often feature depictions of angels, saints, and scenes from liturgical traditions, creating a sacred ambiance that complements the church's rituals and ceremonies.

Educational Insights and Guided Tours:

Enhance your understanding through educational insights and guided tours offered within the exhibition. Knowledgeable guides provide historical context, artistic analysis, and theological perspectives, deepening your appreciation for the cultural and spiritual significance of the stained glass. Engage in discussions and ask questions to enrich your experience.

Community Engagement Projects:

Discover community engagement projects that involve local artists, schools, or congregants in the creation or restoration of stained glass. These projects foster a sense of communal pride and connection, infusing the stained glass tradition with contemporary expressions of creativity and collaboration.

Interactive Workshops and Demonstrations:

Participate in interactive workshops and demonstrations that offer hands-on experiences with stained glass techniques. Whether it's learning about the process of creating a stained glass window or trying your hand at glass cutting, these activities provide a tactile and immersive dimension to your visit.

Seasonal Displays and Liturgical Themes:

Experience the changing beauty of stained glass through seasonal displays and liturgical themes. Some windows may take on different hues or be adorned with seasonal motifs, aligning with the church calendar and liturgical seasons. Witness the adaptability of stained glass in reflecting the cyclical nature of worship and spirituality.

Musical Accompaniment and Evensong Services:

Elevate your experience with musical accompaniment and attendance at Evensong services. The acoustics of the church, combined with the visual splendor of stained glass, create a multisensory encounter that engages both the auditory and visual senses. Immerse yourself in the spiritual ambiance enhanced by the harmonies of choral music.

Reflection Areas and Prayer Spaces:

Take advantage of designated reflection areas and prayer spaces within the church. These quiet corners invite visitors to pause, reflect, and absorb the spiritual energy emanating from the stained glass. Whether you seek a moment of solitude or collective worship, these spaces enhance the contemplative atmosphere.

The St. Edward's Church Stained Glass Exhibition offers a transcendent encounter with the divine expressed through the artistry of stained glass. As you traverse the sacred space adorned with these radiant windows, you not only witness the skill of artisans but also connect with the spiritual narratives that have been woven into the very fabric of St. Edward's Church.

CREATE YOUR STAINED GLASS ART WORKSHOP

Embark on a hands-on artistic journey with the "Create Your Stained Glass Art Workshop," a unique and immersive experience that invites participants to explore the mesmerizing world of stained glass creation. This workshop combines education, creativity, and craftsmanship, allowing individuals to design and craft their own stained glass masterpiece under the guidance of skilled instructors.

Introduction to Stained Glass Art:

Begin the workshop with an introduction to the rich history and artistic traditions of stained glass. Participants gain insights into the evolution of this ancient craft, exploring its cultural significance and the transformative power of colored light through glass.

Basic Principles of Stained Glass Design:

Learn the fundamental principles of stained glass design, including color theory, pattern creation, and the interplay of light and glass.

Instructors guide participants in understanding the importance of these principles in creating visually stunning and harmonious stained glass compositions.

Selection of Materials:

Explore the variety of materials used in stained glass art, from different types of glass to leading, solder, and other essential tools. Participants have the opportunity to feel and examine the textures, colors, and characteristics of various glass options available for their projects.

Tools of the Trade:

Familiarize yourself with the tools used in stained glass craftsmanship. Instructors demonstrate the proper use of glass cutters, grinders, soldering irons, and other specialized tools. Participants receive hands-on guidance to ensure they feel comfortable and confident using these tools during the creative process.

Safety Protocols:

Prioritize safety with a comprehensive overview of safety protocols in stained glass work. Participants learn about protective gear, proper ventilation, and safe handling of tools to create a secure and enjoyable workshop environment.

Design Development Session:

Engage in a design development session where participants sketch and conceptualize their stained glass projects. Instructors provide guidance on translating ideas into feasible designs, considering factors such as scale, complexity, and visual impact.

Color Palette Exploration:

Explore a diverse color palette of stained glass options. Participants experiment with different combinations of hues, tints, and textures to create a customized color scheme that aligns with their artistic vision. This session encourages creativity and personal expression in design choices.

Pattern Construction Techniques:

Learn pattern construction techniques, including the use of templates and traditional lead came or copper foil methods. Instructors guide participants through the process of transferring their designs onto the glass, ensuring precision and accuracy in pattern creation.

Glass Cutting Mastery:

Master the art of glass cutting with hands-on practice. Participants develop proficiency in scoring and breaking glass pieces according to their chosen patterns. Instructors offer tips for achieving clean, precise cuts and overcoming common challenges in the glass cutting process.

Copper Foil or Lead Came Application:

Choose between the copper foil or lead came technique for assembling stained glass pieces. Instructors provide step-by-step instructions on wrapping and soldering copper foil or constructing lead came channels. Participants experience the unique characteristics of each method and make informed choices based on their artistic preferences.

Soldering and Flux Application:

Delve into the intricacies of soldering as participants join their stained glass pieces together. Instructors demonstrate proper soldering techniques, including the application of flux and achieving smooth, consistent solder lines. This stage brings the individual glass elements into a cohesive and structurally sound artwork.

Cleaning and Finishing Touches:

Explore the cleaning and finishing processes to enhance the appearance of the stained glass creation. Participants learn methods for removing excess flux, polishing the glass surfaces, and ensuring a polished, professional finish to their completed projects.

Grouting and Final Presentation:

Conclude the workshop with a session on grouting and final presentation. Participants apply grout to fill the spaces between glass pieces, adding texture and depth to their creations. Instructors provide tips on selecting grout colors that complement the overall design. Each participant leaves with a finished stained glass artwork ready for display.

Group Reflection and Feedback:

Foster a sense of community and collaboration with a group reflection session. Participants share their experiences, insights, and challenges encountered during the workshop. Instructors provide constructive feedback, celebrating individual achievements and highlighting the diversity of creative expressions within the group.

Take-Home Kit and Resources:

Receive a take-home kit containing essential tools and materials, allowing participants to continue exploring stained glass art beyond the workshop. Instructors provide additional resources, including recommended reading materials, online tutorials, and local suppliers for those eager to further refine their skills.

The "Create Your Stained Glass Art Workshop" not only offers participants the opportunity to admire stained glass but empowers them to become creators of their own artistic masterpieces. Through a blend of education, hands-on practice, and artistic expression, this workshop sparks a newfound appreciation for the craftsmanship and beauty inherent in the world of stained glass artistry.

LITERARY HERITAGE

JANE AUSTEN TRAIL IN CHAWTON

Immerse yourself in the world of one of England's literary icons, Jane Austen, by exploring the Jane Austen Trail in Chawton. This enchanting trail offers a glimpse into the life and inspirations of the renowned author, allowing you to walk in her footsteps and discover the settings that influenced some of her most beloved works.

Chawton Cottage:

Begin your journey at Chawton Cottage, the former home of Jane Austen. This charming red-brick house, now known as Jane Austen's House Museum, preserves the rooms where she wrote and revised her novels, including "Pride and Prejudice" and "Emma." Explore the quaint garden that served as a source of inspiration for her writing.

Chawton House Library:

Visit Chawton House Library, a grand Elizabethan manor located near Chawton Cottage. This historic estate was owned by Jane Austen's brother, Edward Knight. The library houses an impressive collection of early women's writing, reflecting the literary context in which Austen lived.

St. Nicholas' Church:

Explore St. Nicholas' Church, where Jane Austen and her family attended services. The churchyard contains the graves of several Austen family members, providing a serene setting to reflect on their contributions to literature and the community.

Jane Austen's Writing Table:

Marvel at Jane Austen's writing table, a treasured artifact displayed in the museum. This small, portable writing desk holds historical significance as the place where Austen penned her novels, showcasing the modest yet powerful tools of a literary genius.

Chawton Village:

Stroll through the picturesque village of Chawton, which retains its 18th-century charm. The village features quintessential English cottages, hedged pathways, and rustic beauty, offering a glimpse into the backdrop of Jane Austen's daily life.

Chawton Village Stores:

Visit Chawton Village Stores, formerly a bakehouse, where Jane Austen would send her characters to purchase goods in her novels. The store's authentic charm and historical connections make it a delightful stop on the trail.

The Greyfriar Pub:

Experience a touch of local hospitality at The Greyfriar Pub. This establishment has its own literary significance, as it is believed that Jane Austen's brother, Edward Knight, would occasionally stop here. Enjoy a meal in the same ambiance that once welcomed the Austen family.

Chawton House Gardens:

Wander through the beautifully landscaped gardens surrounding Chawton House. The gardens offer a peaceful retreat and may have inspired Jane Austen as she found solace and inspiration in the natural beauty that surrounded her.

Jane Austen Memorial Bench:

Pay homage to Jane Austen at the memorial bench located near her former home. This serene spot provides an opportunity for quiet contemplation and reflection on the enduring legacy of the beloved author.

Chawton to Alton Circular Walk:

Embark on the Chawton to Alton Circular Walk, a scenic route that captures the idyllic countryside that Jane Austen would have traversed. This circular walk provides glimpses of Hampshire's landscapes and offers a deeper connection to the natural settings that inspired Austen's novels.

Literary Events and Festivals:

Check for literary events and festivals that may coincide with your visit to Chawton. The village often hosts events celebrating Jane Austen's works, providing an immersive experience for enthusiasts and fostering a sense of community around her literary legacy.

Chawton Woods and Footpaths:

Explore the footpaths and wooded areas around Chawton, imagining the leisurely walks that Jane Austen might have taken. The rustic beauty of the woods adds a contemplative aspect to your journey, connecting you with the nature that Austen so often incorporated into her novels.

Period Costume Displays:

Delight in displays of period costumes at the museum, allowing you to visualize the attire worn during Jane Austen's time. Period costume exhibits provide a vivid glimpse into the social context that influenced Austen's characters and narratives.

Literary Workshops and Talks:

Participate in literary workshops or talks organized in Chawton. Engaging with Austen scholars and enthusiasts provides an intellectual dimension to your exploration, deepening your understanding of Jane Austen's literary contributions.

Jane Austen's Birthday Celebrations:

If your visit aligns with Jane Austen's birthday in December, partake in the festivities held in Chawton. Celebrations often include period-themed events, readings, and gatherings that commemorate the author's enduring influence.

Jane Austen's Garden Tea Party:

Attend a Jane Austen-themed garden tea party if available during your visit. Such events capture the elegance and social customs of Austen's era, allowing you to experience a taste of the refined gatherings depicted in her novels.

Literary Souvenirs:

Conclude your Jane Austen Trail with literary souvenirs from the museum's gift shop. Whether it's a reproduction of a writing quill or a copy of one of Austen's novels, these keepsakes serve as reminders of your journey into the world of this literary luminary.

The Jane Austen Trail in Chawton is not merely a historical exploration but a journey into the literary landscapes that shaped one of the world's most beloved authors. As you traverse the village and its surroundings, you step into the pages of Austen's novels, gaining a profound appreciation for the settings, inspirations, and daily life that influenced her timeless literary creations.

ROAM THE INSPIRATIONAL SETTINGS OF C.S. LEWIS

Embark on a literary pilgrimage through the inspirational settings that fueled the imagination of C.S. Lewis, the prolific author of "The Chronicles of Narnia" and other timeless works. This journey takes you to places that played a significant role in Lewis's life, providing insights into the sources of his creativity and the magic that shaped his literary legacy.

The Kilns:

Begin your exploration at The Kilns, C.S. Lewis's former residence in Oxford. This sprawling house, surrounded by picturesque gardens, served as Lewis's home for over three decades. Tour the rooms where Lewis wrote many of his iconic works and gain a glimpse into the daily life that influenced his literary creations.

Magdalen College, Oxford:

Visit Magdalen College, where C.S. Lewis taught as a fellow and tutor for nearly three decades. Stroll through the historic grounds and the majestic Magdalen Tower, absorbing the academic atmosphere that Lewis experienced and drawing inspiration from the architectural beauty of the college.

Addison's Walk:

Wander along Addison's Walk, a scenic path that traces the banks of the River Cherwell at Magdalen College. This tranquil walkway, a favorite of Lewis, offers a serene escape and invites contemplation, providing a glimpse into the natural settings that influenced his thoughts and writings.

The Eagle and Child Pub:

Stop by The Eagle and Child pub in Oxford, fondly known as the "Bird and Baby." This historic watering hole was a regular meeting place for the Inklings, a literary group that included C.S. Lewis and J.R.R. Tolkien. Capture the essence of the conversations and camaraderie that flourished within these walls.

St. Mary's Church, Headington:

Explore St. Mary's Church in Headington, where C.S. Lewis is buried alongside his brother, Warren. The simple gravestones in the churchyard mark the final resting place of the beloved author. Take a moment for reflection and pay homage to Lewis's literary contributions.

Oxford Botanic Garden:

Find inspiration in the Oxford Botanic Garden, a lush and vibrant space that Lewis frequented. The diverse plant life and tranquil surroundings may evoke the magical landscapes of Narnia, providing a visual link between the natural world and Lewis's fantastical realms.

Belfast:

Venture to Belfast, Northern Ireland, where C.S. Lewis spent his early years. Explore the city's streets, visit his childhood home, and absorb the urban landscapes that left an indelible mark on his imaginative storytelling.

Dundela Avenue, Belfast:

Walk along Dundela Avenue in Belfast, the location of the Lewis family home, known as "Little Lea." This residential street and the surrounding neighborhood influenced Lewis's early experiences and may have shaped his perceptions of home and adventure.

Strandtown Primary School:

Visit Strandtown Primary School, where C.S. Lewis began his formal education. The school's architecture and surroundings provide insights into the early educational environment that nurtured Lewis's intellectual curiosity.

Dunluce Castle:

Explore Dunluce Castle on the Causeway Coast in Northern Ireland. While not directly associated with Lewis, the dramatic ruins and coastal vistas may evoke the awe-inspiring landscapes featured in Narnia. Let the castle's history and surroundings spark your imagination.

East Belfast Library:

Delve into East Belfast Library, where a young C.S. Lewis discovered a wealth of books that fueled his love for literature. The library's role in fostering Lewis's early literary passions adds a layer of significance to this unassuming space.

Cair Paravel:

Visit locations that resemble the landscapes of Narnia. While not specific settings that directly inspired Lewis, places with vast woodlands, ancient ruins, or majestic landscapes may evoke the enchanting world of Narnia and provide a visual connection to Lewis's fantastical realms.

Local Nature Reserves:

Immerse yourself in local nature reserves or wooded areas, drawing inspiration from the natural settings that often played a pivotal role in C.S. Lewis's storytelling. Allow the sights, sounds, and scents of these landscapes to transport you to the imaginative realms of Narnia.

CS Lewis Square, Belfast:

Visit CS Lewis Square in Belfast, a public space dedicated to the author. The square features sculptures and public art inspired by Lewis's works, providing a tangible and artistic celebration of his literary legacy.

Narnia Themed Exhibitions:

Seek out Narnia-themed exhibitions or displays in local museums or literary events. These showcases often feature artifacts, illustrations, and interactive elements that bring the magic of Narnia to life, offering a unique and immersive experience for fans of C.S. Lewis.

Local Bookstores:

Explore local bookstores in Belfast and Oxford. These bookshops may carry editions of C.S. Lewis's works, allowing you to acquire literary treasures and continue the journey into the imaginative worlds crafted by this literary luminary.

Literary Events and Lectures:

Check for literary events and lectures focused on C.S. Lewis. Universities, libraries, or cultural organizations may host talks and discussions that delve into Lewis's life, works, and enduring influence, providing an enriching dimension to your exploration.

Roaming the inspirational settings of C.S. Lewis is not just a physical journey but a pilgrimage into the landscapes of imagination that shaped one of the greatest storytellers of the 20th century. As you tread the paths he walked and visit the places that left an indelible mark on his soul, you'll find a deeper appreciation for the magic that continues to captivate readers across generations.

WRITING RETREAT IN THE COTSWOLD COUNTRYSIDE

Embark on a transformative writing retreat in the picturesque Cotswold countryside, where the rolling hills, charming villages, and timeless beauty create an inspiring backdrop for writers seeking solace and creativity. This literary escape is designed to provide a harmonious blend of tranquility, inspiration, and the rich heritage of the Cotswolds to nurture your writing endeavors.

Charming Accommodation:

Settle into a charming cottage or a historic inn nestled amidst the Cotswold landscape. The accommodation, adorned with rustic charm and modern comforts, serves as your writing haven, offering a peaceful retreat after each day of literary exploration.

Secluded Writing Spaces:

Discover secluded writing spaces within your chosen accommodation or venture into the serene outdoors. Whether it's a cozy study with a fireplace or a garden nook overlooking rolling hills, these spaces are designed to foster focus and creativity, providing an intimate setting for your writing sessions.

Countryside Strolls for Inspiration:

Embark on leisurely strolls through the countryside, drawing inspiration from the idyllic landscapes. The meandering footpaths, flower-filled meadows, and ancient woodlands offer a sensory experience that can stimulate your imagination and infuse your writing with the essence of the Cotswolds.

Village Exploration for Local Flavor:

Explore nearby villages to absorb the local flavor and heritage. Wander through cobbled streets lined with honey-colored cottages, visit historic churches, and engage with the vibrant community. The unique character of each village becomes a wellspring of inspiration, enriching your writing with the cultural tapestry of the Cotswolds.

Literary Landmarks Tour:

Take a literary landmarks tour, visiting places associated with renowned authors who found inspiration in the Cotswolds. From the homes of Laurie Lee to the landscapes that inspired J.R.R. Tolkien, each landmark unveils layers of literary heritage, connecting you with the writers who once sought solace and creativity in this region.

Tea-Time Writing Retreats:

Indulge in tea-time writing retreats, taking breaks to savor traditional afternoon tea in cozy tearooms. The ritual of tea, accompanied by delectable treats, provides moments of relaxation and reflection, allowing your mind to wander and return to your writing with renewed focus.

Historic Libraries and Bookshops:

Immerse yourself in historic libraries and quaint bookshops that dot the Cotswold villages. The aroma of old books and the hushed ambiance create an intimate setting for contemplation. Engage with the literary treasures and let the written words of others kindle your own creative spark.

Writing Workshops with Local Authors:

Participate in writing workshops led by local authors who call the Cotswolds home. These sessions, set against the backdrop of the countryside, offer valuable insights, feedback, and a sense of camaraderie with fellow writers. The workshops become a communal space to share ideas and refine your craft.

Artistic Retreats in Nature:

Integrate artistic retreats into your writing experience, incorporating elements of nature into your creative process. Whether it's sketching in a garden or capturing the landscape through photography, these artistic endeavors complement your writing, fostering a multidimensional approach to creativity.

Cotswold Folklore and Legends:

Immerse yourself in Cotswold folklore and legends that have been woven into the fabric of the region. From ancient tales to local myths, these narratives can serve as thematic threads in your writing, adding a touch of mystique and cultural depth to your literary creations.

Seasonal Inspirations:

Embrace the changing seasons as a source of inspiration. Whether it's the blossoming flowers of spring, the vibrant colors of autumn, or the cozy ambiance of winter, each season brings its own unique charm to the Cotswold countryside, influencing the mood and tone of your writing.

Evening Fireside Writing Sessions:

Conclude your days with evening fireside writing sessions. The crackling warmth of a fireplace, paired with the gentle sounds of the countryside, creates a soothing ambiance for introspective writing. Allow the tranquility of the Cotswolds to infuse your work with a sense of peace and reflection.

Local Farmers' Markets for Culinary Inspiration:

Explore local farmers' markets for culinary inspiration. Engage with farmers, sample fresh produce, and immerse yourself in the gastronomic delights of the Cotswolds. The sensory experience of flavors and aromas can become a muse for your writing, infusing your narratives with a rich tapestry of tastes.

Cotswold Nature Writing:

Engage in Cotswold nature writing, capturing the essence of the landscape through your words. Whether it's a sunrise over rolling hills, the rustle of leaves in a hidden grove, or the call of birds in the early morning, let the natural world become a vivid character in your literary compositions.

Public Readings in Village Halls:

Share your work with the local community through public readings in village halls or community spaces. The intimate setting allows you to connect with your audience, receive feedback, and create a sense of literary community in the heart of the Cotswolds.

Yoga and Meditation Retreats:

Incorporate yoga and meditation retreats into your writing sojourn. The Cotswold countryside provides a serene backdrop for mindfulness practices, offering moments of tranquility and mental clarity to enhance your writing process.

Cotswold Literary Festivals:

Time your retreat to coincide with Cotswold literary festivals. These events celebrate the written word, bringing together authors, readers, and literary enthusiasts. Attend panel discussions, book signings, and engage with the vibrant literary community that thrives in the Cotswolds.

A writing retreat in the Cotswold countryside transcends the act of writing; it becomes a holistic experience that intertwines nature, culture, and creativity. As you immerse yourself in the timeless beauty of this region, your writing journey unfolds not only as words on paper but as a profound exploration of self, place, and the rich literary heritage that defines the Cotswolds.

GHOST TOURS AND HAUNTED HISTORY

SPOOKY EVENING TOUR OF WOODCHESTER MANSION

Embark on a spine-tingling journey into the spectral realm with the "Spooky Evening Tour of Woodchester Mansion," a ghostly adventure that unfolds within the historic and enigmatic walls of Woodchester Mansion. As dusk descends, participants are immersed in an eerie atmosphere, exploring the mysterious corridors and dimly lit rooms while unraveling tales of paranormal encounters, haunted history, and the lingering spirits that inhabit this hauntingly beautiful mansion.

Introduction to Woodchester Mansion:

Begin the evening with an atmospheric introduction to Woodchester Mansion, a Victorian Gothic masterpiece nestled within the secluded Woodchester Park. The guide sets the tone for the ghostly adventure, sharing historical insights and intriguing anecdotes about the mansion's construction, its enigmatic past, and the rumored paranormal activity that has captured the imaginations of visitors.

Evening Arrival and Atmosphere:

Arrive as the sun sets, casting long shadows across the mansion's grand facade. The evening atmosphere adds an extra layer of mystery to the surroundings, setting the stage for an immersive and atmospheric ghost tour. Dim lighting and carefully orchestrated ambience enhance the eerie ambiance, creating an environment conducive to supernatural storytelling.

Guided Tour Through Darkened Halls:

Venture into the mansion's darkened halls and shadowy chambers under the guidance of an expert storyteller and guide. As participants traverse the labyrinthine corridors, the guide shares tales of reported ghostly encounters, unexplained phenomena, and the historical events that contribute to the mansion's haunted reputation.

Haunted Hotspots and Paranormal Stories:

Explore haunted hotspots within Woodchester Mansion, stopping at key locations where paranormal activity has been reported. The guide reveals chilling tales associated with each location, recounting firsthand experiences and sharing accounts of encounters with apparitions, mysterious sounds, and unexplained phenomena that defy rational explanation.

The Chapel's Ghostly Presence:

Stand in hushed reverence within the mansion's hauntingly beautiful chapel, known for its reported ghostly presence. The guide delves into the chapel's history, its architectural significance, and the tales of spectral sightings that have been recounted by those who have dared to enter this sacred yet mysterious space.

Secluded Gardens and Ghostly Residues:

Explore the secluded gardens surrounding Woodchester Mansion, where ghostly residues and eerie phenomena are said to manifest. The guide shares stories of paranormal occurrences in the outdoor spaces, creating an immersive experience that extends beyond the mansion's walls and into the atmospheric natural surroundings.

Spiritualism and Victorian Seances:

Gain insights into the Victorian fascination with spiritualism and the practice of seances. Learn how the historical context of the era influenced beliefs in the afterlife and paranormal communication. The guide discusses the role of spiritualism within Woodchester Mansion's history and its impact on reported ghostly activities.

EVP Sessions and Paranormal Investigations:

Engage in electronic voice phenomenon (EVP) sessions and paranormal investigations led by experienced ghost hunters. Participants have the opportunity to use specialized equipment to capture potential paranormal audio recordings and gather firsthand experiences of the unexplained. This interactive element adds a dynamic and immersive layer to the ghost tour.

Supernatural Photography Opportunities:

Seize the opportunity for supernatural photography as participants explore the mansion's dimly lit interiors and eerie surroundings. Guides share tips on capturing potential paranormal anomalies, encouraging participants to document their own ghostly encounters through the lens of their cameras.

Interactive Paranormal Experiments:

Participate in interactive paranormal experiments designed to heighten the ghostly experience. From pendulum dowsing to divination tools, participants engage in activities that draw upon historical practices associated with paranormal investigations, enhancing the sense of connection to the spiritual energies believed to inhabit Woodchester Mansion.

Encounter with Residual Energies:

Experience the palpable sense of residual energies within Woodchester Mansion. The guide facilitates moments of stillness and reflection, allowing participants to tune into the atmospheric vibrations and connect with the lingering energies that are said to remain from the mansion's storied past.

Conclusion and Haunting Reflections:

Conclude the spooky evening tour with haunting reflections and a debriefing session. Participants have the opportunity to share their experiences, ask questions, and reflect on the ghostly encounters within Woodchester Mansion. The guide provides additional insights into the history of paranormal investigations at the mansion and the ongoing quest to unravel its mysteries.

Haunted Merchandise and Commemorative Items:

Explore haunted merchandise and commemorative items available for purchase. From ghostly souvenirs to books documenting the haunted history of Woodchester Mansion, participants can acquire mementos to commemorate their chilling journey into the supernatural.

The Spooky Evening Tour of Woodchester Mansion offers a captivating blend of history, mystery, and paranormal exploration, providing participants with an unforgettable and eerie encounter with the spectral side of this Victorian Gothic marvel. As shadows deepen and ghostly tales come to life, the mansion's haunted history unfolds, leaving participants with an indelible impression of the supernatural mysteries that linger within its walls.

HAUNTED PUB CRAWL IN STOW-ON-THE-WOLD

Embark on a chilling and spirited journey through the historic streets of Stow-on-the-Wold with the "Haunted Pub Crawl," an otherworldly adventure that combines the charm of centuries-old pubs with tales of restless spirits, eerie encounters, and the haunted history that lurks within this picturesque Cotswold town.

Meeting Point at Dusk:

Gather at a designated meeting point as dusk descends over Stow-on-the-Wold, creating an atmospheric backdrop for the haunted pub crawl. The guide, a seasoned storyteller with a penchant for the paranormal, welcomes participants and sets the stage for an evening of ghostly tales.

Introduction to Stow-on-the-Wold's Haunted Past:

Begin the haunted pub crawl with an introduction to Stow-on-the-Wold's haunted past. The guide shares historical insights into the town's rich tapestry of legends, mysterious occurrences, and ghostly apparitions that have left an indelible mark on its quaint streets and centuries-old buildings.

Haunted Pubs with Darkened Interiors:

Visit a series of haunted pubs with darkened interiors that echo with the whispers of centuries gone by. Each pub on the crawl has its own spectral stories and ghostly lore. The guide leads participants through creaking doorways and atmospheric settings, setting the scene for spine-tingling encounters.

Ghostly Tales of Pubs Past:

Settle into the historic pubs, where participants are regaled with ghostly tales associated with each establishment. From spectral patrons to haunted corners, the guide paints vivid narratives of the supernatural occurrences that have been reported by patrons, staff, and visitors over the years.

The Phantom Drinker:

Hear the legend of the phantom drinker who is said to linger in one of the pubs, perpetually raising a spectral glass in a toast that transcends the boundaries between the living and the departed. The guide weaves a tale of this ethereal imbiber, recounting encounters and mysterious happenings witnessed by those who have crossed paths with the apparition.

Haunted Pub Architecture and History:

Delve into the architectural and historical aspects of the haunted pubs. The guide provides insights into the construction, renovations, and past uses of these establishments, shedding light on how the passage of time has contributed to the lingering energies and spectral presences within.

The Tragic Tale of the Tavern Maid:

Uncover the tragic tale of a tavern maid whose spirit is said to roam one of the pubs in perpetual search of a lost love. The guide narrates the heart-wrenching story, sharing accounts of encounters with the melancholic apparition and exploring the emotional resonance that persists within the pub's walls.

EVP Sessions in Haunted Corners:

Engage in electronic voice phenomenon (EVP) sessions in the haunted corners of the pubs. Participants use recording devices to capture potential paranormal voices and sounds that may go unnoticed by the human ear. The guide encourages active participation, creating an interactive and immersive experience for those seeking to connect with the supernatural.

Ghostly Apparitions and Poltergeist Tales:

Encounter tales of ghostly apparitions and poltergeist activity reported in various pubs along the crawl. From spectral figures that materialize in dark corners to unexplained movements of objects, participants are regaled with stories that blur the lines between the natural and supernatural realms.

Interactive Spirit Communication Tools:

Explore interactive spirit communication tools such as dowsing rods or pendulums under the guidance of the paranormal expert. Participants have the opportunity to use these tools to seek answers to questions or attempt to establish a connection with the ethereal energies believed to inhabit the pubs.

Haunted Courtyards and Alleyways:

Navigate haunted courtyards and narrow alleyways that connect the haunted pubs. The guide shares tales of spectral sightings and eerie phenomena that extend beyond the confines of the pubs, creating a sense of continuity in the haunted history of Stow-on-the-Wold.

Conclusion at the Witching Hour:

Conclude the haunted pub crawl as the night deepens and the witching hour approaches. Participants gather for a final round of ghostly tales and reflections on the spine-tingling experiences encountered during the evening. The guide leaves participants with lingering thoughts about the paranormal mysteries that enshroud Stow-on-the-Wold.

Optional Nightcap and Casual Discussion:

Opt for an optional nightcap at one of the haunted pubs, providing participants with the opportunity for casual discussion and sharing of personal experiences. The guide remains available for questions, anecdotes, and informal conversations about the supernatural aspects of Stow-on-the-Wold.

The Haunted Pub Crawl in Stow-on-the-Wold offers a bewitching blend of history, folklore, and paranormal exploration. As participants navigate the haunted pubs and dimly lit corners, they are transported into a realm where the past and the present intersect, revealing the spectral stories that continue to echo through the ancient streets of this charming Cotswold town.

COTSWOLD GHOST STORIES BY CANDLELIGHT

Immerse yourself in an evening of eerie enchantment with "Cotswold Ghost Stories by Candlelight," a hauntingly atmospheric experience that unfolds within the historic and mystical landscapes of the Cotswolds. Guided by flickering candlelight, participants embark on a journey through the spectral tales and supernatural mysteries that have left an indelible mark on the hauntingly beautiful corners of this enchanting region.

Gathering at Dusk in a Historic Setting:

Begin the evening by gathering at a historic setting as the sun sets, casting long shadows and setting the stage for a night of spine-tingling tales. The guide, a master storyteller with a penchant for the paranormal, welcomes participants to an atmospheric environment illuminated solely by the soft glow of candles.

Introduction to Cotswold's Haunted History:

Set the mood with an introduction to the haunted history of the Cotswolds. The guide shares tales of ghostly apparitions, lingering spirits, and the mysterious folklore that pervades the ancient villages and landscapes. Participants are encouraged to embrace the mystical ambiance as they prepare for an unforgettable journey into the unknown.

Candlelit Walk Through Historic Streets:

Embark on a candlelit walk through historic streets, winding pathways, and cobblestone alleys. The guide leads participants through the heart of the Cotswolds, where centuries-old buildings and charming architecture provide the perfect backdrop for ghostly narratives. The soft glow of candles enhances the enchanting atmosphere.

Haunted Villages and Their Stories:

Explore haunted villages within the Cotswolds, each with its own set of ghostly tales waiting to be unveiled. As participants stroll through quaint streets and past medieval structures, the guide narrates stories of spectral sightings, paranormal phenomena, and the mysterious events that have left an indelible imprint on these timeless landscapes.

Candlelit Visits to Mysterious Locations:

Make candlelit visits to mysterious locations associated with ghostly occurrences. The guide strategically unveils stories at specific spots, creating an immersive experience that allows participants to connect with the haunted narratives while surrounded by the tangible echoes of the past.

Phantom Figures and Ethereal Apparitions:

Encounter tales of phantom figures and ethereal apparitions said to wander the Cotswold villages. The guide shares accounts of ghostly encounters witnessed by locals and visitors alike, bringing to life the spectral inhabitants that are believed to linger in the shadows of centuries-old buildings.

Candlelit Cemetery Exploration:

Enter a candlelit cemetery where the guide reveals tales of restless souls and haunted graves. Participants navigate the sacred grounds, hearing stories of unexplained phenomena, mysterious tombstones, and the eerie occurrences that have led to rumors of supernatural activity within the silent confines of the cemetery.

Interactive Ghostly Experiences:

Engage in interactive ghostly experiences guided by the storyteller. Participants may partake in activities that invite connection with the paranormal, creating a sense of shared exploration and a heightened awareness of the mystical energies believed to inhabit the Cotswold landscapes.

Historical Anecdotes of the Unexplained:

Delve into historical anecdotes of the unexplained, showcasing how the Cotswolds have been steeped in mystery throughout the ages. The guide shares stories that blend historical facts with supernatural elements, providing participants with a captivating and nuanced perspective on the region's haunted heritage.

Haunted Manor Houses and Their Legends:

Hear tales of haunted manor houses and their lingering legends. As participants approach grand estates with flickering candlelight, the guide reveals stories of ghostly inhabitants, tragic love stories, and the mysterious occurrences that have contributed to the haunted reputations of these stately homes.

Candlelit Séance Experience:

Engage in a candlelit séance experience led by the guide. Participants gather in a carefully chosen location where the guide creates an atmosphere conducive to spiritual communication. The séance adds a touch of mysticism, inviting participants to be open to the possibility of connecting with the unseen.

Conclusion with Haunting Reflections:

Conclude the evening with haunting reflections as participants gather in a designated space. The guide invites participants to share their experiences, ask questions, and reflect on the ghostly tales encountered by candlelight. The soft glow of candles provides an intimate setting for lingering thoughts and discussions.

Optional Candlelit Refreshments and Socializing:

Opt for optional candlelit refreshments and socializing in a historic setting. Participants can enjoy warm beverages or snacks as they share their experiences, exchange ghost stories, and soak in the lingering enchantment of the evening. The guide remains available for informal discussions and further exploration of the haunting narratives.

"Cotswold Ghost Stories by Candlelight" offers a mesmerizing blend of history, folklore, and spectral exploration. As participants navigate the candlelit landscapes and absorb the chilling tales, they become enveloped in the timeless mystique of the Cotswolds, where the line between the living and the departed blurs in the flickering glow of candlelight.

RELAXATION AND WELLNESS

SPA DAY IN A COTSWOLD RETREAT

Embark on a rejuvenating journey of self-care and tranquility with a Spa Day in a Cotswold Retreat. Nestled in the heart of the picturesque Cotswolds, this retreat offers a serene oasis where you can escape the hustle and bustle, indulge in luxurious treatments, and immerse yourself in a world of relaxation and wellness.

Arrival at the Cotswold Retreat:

Begin your spa day with a warm welcome as you arrive at the Cotswold Retreat. The serene ambiance, surrounded by nature's beauty, sets the tone for a day dedicated to relaxation and rejuvenation.

Cotswold-Inspired Spa Decor:

Immerse yourself in the Cotswold-inspired spa decor that reflects the region's charm and tranquility. Earthy tones, natural materials, and subtle nods to the local landscape create an inviting space that encourages a sense of calm and well-being.

Consultation with Spa Professionals:

Engage in a personalized consultation with spa professionals. Discuss your preferences, any specific concerns, and desired outcomes for the day. This ensures that your spa experience is tailored to meet your individual needs and goals.

Relaxation Lounge and Herbal Teas:

Unwind in the relaxation lounge adorned with comfortable furnishings. Sip on soothing herbal teas as you transition into a state of relaxation, allowing the gentle ambiance to prepare you for the pampering that lies ahead.

Hydrotherapy and Thermal Experiences:

Immerse yourself in hydrotherapy and thermal experiences that promote relaxation and detoxification. Indulge in a journey through various heat and water therapies, such as saunas, steam rooms, and hydrotherapy pools, preparing your body for the upcoming spa treatments.

Signature Cotswold Retreat Massage:

Experience the Signature Cotswold Retreat Massage, a bespoke treatment that combines traditional massage techniques with locally inspired elements. The skilled therapists use aromatic oils infused with botanicals from the Cotswolds, ensuring a sensory journey that promotes relaxation and rejuvenation.

Cotswold Honey and Lavender Body Wrap:

Indulge in a luxurious Cotswold Honey and Lavender Body Wrap. This nourishing treatment utilizes locally sourced honey and lavender to hydrate and soothe the skin. As you cocoon in warmth, the calming scents transport you to the lavender fields and honey gardens of the Cotswolds.

Cotswold Garden Facial:

Treat your skin to a rejuvenating Cotswold Garden Facial. Tailored to your skin type, this facial incorporates botanical extracts inspired by the local flora. The therapist's skilled hands and the therapeutic scents leave your skin radiant and refreshed.

Aromatherapy Relaxation Room:

Bask in the tranquility of the aromatherapy relaxation room. Soft lighting, calming scents, and comfortable loungers create an atmosphere of serenity, allowing you to extend the benefits of your spa treatments while taking moments of quiet reflection.

Cotswold-Inspired Cuisine:

Delight your palate with Cotswold-inspired cuisine at the spa's restaurant. Savor dishes crafted with locally sourced ingredients, ensuring a culinary experience that complements the overall theme of well-being and connection to the region.

Yoga or Meditation Session:

Engage in a gentle yoga or meditation session to further enhance your sense of relaxation. The peaceful surroundings of the Cotswold Retreat provide an ideal setting for mindfulness practices, allowing you to connect with your inner self and the natural beauty of the surroundings.

Guided Nature Walk or Garden Stroll:

Take a guided nature walk or leisurely stroll through the retreat's gardens. Connecting with nature amplifies the benefits of your spa day, providing a holistic experience that rejuvenates both body and soul.

Cotswold-Inspired Souvenirs:

Conclude your spa day by perusing Cotswold-inspired souvenirs at the retreat's boutique. From locally crafted wellness products to spa essentials, these mementos serve as reminders of your rejuvenating day in the heart of the Cotswolds.

Farewell and Continued Wellness:

Bid farewell to the Cotswold Retreat with a sense of renewed well-being. Carry the tranquility and balance you've cultivated into your everyday life, knowing that the serene haven of the Cotswold Retreat awaits whenever you seek a moment of relaxation and wellness.

YOGA RETREAT IN THE COUNTRYSIDE

Embark on a transformative journey of self-discovery and rejuvenation with a Yoga Retreat in the Countryside. Set against the backdrop of the serene and picturesque countryside, this retreat offers a holistic experience that combines the ancient practice of yoga, mindful activities, and a deep connection with nature.

Arrival at the Countryside Yoga Retreat:

Begin your yoga retreat with a warm welcome as you arrive at the tranquil countryside setting. The air is crisp, and the natural surroundings set the stage for a retreat that focuses on relaxation, mindfulness, and personal well-being.

Rustic Yoga Retreat Architecture:

Immerse yourself in the rustic architecture of the yoga retreat. Earthy tones, natural materials, and large windows that frame scenic views create a harmonious blend between the retreat's structure and the idyllic countryside landscape.

Yoga Pavilion Amidst Nature:

Discover the yoga pavilion nestled amidst nature. Surrounded by trees, open fields, or rolling hills, the pavilion provides a sacred space for yoga practice, allowing you to connect with the elements and find balance in the embrace of the natural world.

Morning Sunrise Yoga Sessions:

Awaken your senses with morning sunrise yoga sessions. Practice gentle asanas and sun salutations as the sun bathes the countryside in a warm glow. The tranquility of the early morning enhances the meditative aspects of your yoga practice.

Guided Meditation by the Countryside Stream:

Experience guided meditation sessions by a peaceful countryside stream. The soothing sounds of flowing water and the rustling leaves create an immersive environment for mindfulness, allowing you to center your thoughts and cultivate inner calm.

Mindful Nature Walks:

Embark on mindful nature walks through the countryside. Engage your senses as you walk among wildflowers, breathe in the fresh air, and absorb the sights and sounds of the natural surroundings. These walks become moving meditations, enhancing your connection with the earth.

Nutrient-Rich Vegetarian Cuisine:

Delight your taste buds with nutrient-rich vegetarian cuisine. The retreat's chefs craft meals using locally sourced, seasonal ingredients. The wholesome and nourishing food complements your yoga practice, promoting a holistic approach to well-being.

Yoga Nidra and Relaxation Workshops:

Participate in Yoga Nidra and relaxation workshops. These sessions guide you through deep relaxation techniques, promoting restorative rest and fostering a sense of tranquility. The retreat encourages a balance between active yoga practice and restful rejuvenation.

Individualized Yoga Instruction:

Receive individualized yoga instruction tailored to your skill level and personal goals. Experienced yoga instructors guide you through postures, alignment, and breathwork, creating a supportive environment for both beginners and experienced practitioners.

Evening Candlelit Yoga Sessions:

Conclude your days with candlelit yoga sessions. The gentle flicker of candles creates an intimate and serene atmosphere, enhancing the restorative nature of the evening practice. The sessions focus on relaxation, gentle stretches, and mindfulness.

Outdoor Yoga Amidst Blossoming Gardens:

Practice yoga amidst blossoming gardens. Whether surrounded by fragrant flowers, lush greenery, or beneath the shade of ancient trees, the outdoor yoga sessions immerse you in the beauty of the countryside, creating a harmonious connection with nature.

Stargazing Meditation Nights:

Embrace the stillness of the countryside with stargazing meditation nights. Lay back under the open sky, allowing the vastness of the cosmos to inspire a sense of wonder and perspective. Guided meditations encourage reflection on the interconnectedness of all things.

Holistic Wellness Workshops:

Engage in holistic wellness workshops that complement your yoga practice. From mindfulness and stress reduction to nutrition and Ayurveda, these workshops offer additional tools for cultivating a balanced and healthy lifestyle.

Farewell Fire Circle Ceremony:

Conclude your yoga retreat with a farewell fire circle ceremony. Gather around a crackling fire, share reflections, and express gratitude for the transformative experience. The circle fosters a sense of community and unity among participants, creating lasting connections forged through shared wellness.

A Yoga Retreat in the Countryside is not just an escape; it's a profound journey of self-care, mindfulness, and connection with the natural world. The retreat invites you to explore the depths of your inner self, find peace in the tranquility of the countryside, and carry the lessons of balance and well-being into your everyday life.

THERMAL BATH EXPERIENCE IN BATH (NEAR COTSWOLDS)

Embark on a luxurious journey of relaxation and rejuvenation with a Thermal Bath Experience in the historic city of Bath, situated near the enchanting Cotswolds. Bath's renowned thermal baths, surrounded by rich history and stunning architecture, provide a unique and indulgent wellness retreat.

Arrival at the Thermal Baths:

Begin your thermal bath experience with a warm welcome as you enter the historic baths. The architecture reflects Bath's Roman and Georgian heritage, setting the scene for a spa day that seamlessly blends tradition with modern luxury.

Roman Baths:

Explore the iconic Roman Baths, a testament to Bath's ancient bathing traditions. Wander through the atmospheric chambers, admire the well-preserved architecture, and learn about the fascinating history of the baths that date back to Roman times.

Modern Thermal Bath Facilities:

Indulge in the modern thermal bath facilities that complement Bath's historic charm. The contemporary design seamlessly integrates with the city's heritage, creating a tranquil environment for your thermal bathing experience.

Mineral-Rich Thermal Pools:

Immerse yourself in the mineral-rich thermal pools that are the centerpiece of the experience. The warm waters, sourced from Bath's natural thermal springs, provide a soothing and therapeutic environment, inviting you to relax and unwind.

Steam Rooms and Saunas:

Enjoy the detoxifying benefits of steam rooms and saunas. These heat experiences complement the thermal baths, promoting circulation, easing muscle tension, and enhancing the overall sense of well-being.

Aromatherapy Showers:

Revitalize your senses with aromatherapy showers. Choose from a variety of scents, each designed to invigorate or relax, as you indulge in a sensory shower experience that complements the healing properties of the thermal waters.

Ice Chambers and Cooling Zones:

Experience the invigorating contrast of ice chambers and cooling zones. These areas provide a refreshing respite, allowing you to cool down between thermal experiences and invigorate your body.

Relaxation Areas with City Views:

Unwind in relaxation areas with panoramic views of the city. These serene spaces provide a tranquil retreat where you can recline and appreciate the historic skyline of Bath, creating a harmonious blend of relaxation and visual delight.

Thermal Bath Treatments:

Enhance your experience with thermal bath treatments. From mineral-rich mud masks to soothing massages, the skilled therapists offer a range of treatments that harness the therapeutic properties of the thermal waters, leaving you feeling rejuvenated.

Rooftop Pool and Sunset Soaks:

Delight in a rooftop pool experience with sunset soaks. As the day transitions into evening, immerse yourself in warm waters on the rooftop, allowing you to relax while enjoying stunning views of Bath's skyline during the magical golden hour.

Cotswold-Inspired Cuisine at the Spa Restaurant:

Indulge in Cotswold-inspired cuisine at the spa's restaurant. Savor nutritious and delectable dishes crafted with locally sourced ingredients, creating a culinary experience that complements your wellness journey.

Yoga and Mindfulness Classes:

Engage in yoga and mindfulness classes offered in the serene surroundings of the thermal baths. These classes provide an opportunity to further enhance your relaxation, focus your mind, and connect with the present moment.

Guided Wellness Workshops:

Participate in guided wellness workshops that offer insights into holistic well-being. From mindfulness practices to nutritional guidance, these workshops provide additional tools for maintaining a balanced and healthy lifestyle.

Bath's Evening Illumination Experience:

Conclude your thermal bath experience by enjoying Bath's evening illumination. As the sun sets and the city lights up, savor the beauty of Bath's architectural treasures from a unique vantage point, creating a serene and unforgettable conclusion to your day of relaxation and wellness.

A Thermal Bath Experience in Bath near the Cotswolds is not just a spa day; it's a journey into the healing waters that have drawn visitors for centuries. It offers a perfect blend of ancient traditions, modern luxury, and the picturesque charm of both Bath and the nearby Cotswolds, ensuring a wellness retreat that rejuvenates both body and spirit.

CAPTURE SCENIC VIEWS

CLIMB BROADWAY TOWER FOR PANORAMIC VISTAS

Elevate your Cotswolds experience by ascending to new heights at Broadway Tower, an iconic vantage point that promises breathtaking panoramic views of the surrounding countryside. Perched atop Fish Hill, near the charming village of Broadway, this historic tower offers an unparalleled opportunity to immerse yourself in the beauty of the Cotswolds.

Arrival at Broadway Tower:

Begin your journey by arriving at the base of Broadway Tower, where the anticipation of the climb is heightened by the tower's imposing presence against the backdrop of the rolling hills.

Climbing the Tower:

Ascend the tower via the spiraling staircase, feeling the resonance of history in the very steps that have been traversed by visitors throughout the centuries.

The gradual ascent adds an element of anticipation, each step revealing a new glimpse of the surrounding landscape.

Historical Significance:

Appreciate the historical significance of Broadway Tower, originally built in the 18th century. Its purpose as a folly, a structure built for ornamentation and viewing, adds a layer of intrigue to your climb.

Architectural Details:

Admire the architectural details of the tower as you ascend. From the honey-hued Cotswold stone to the intricate design elements, the tower itself becomes a captivating focal point.

Intermediate Platforms:

Pause at intermediate platforms along the ascent, allowing you to catch your breath and appreciate partial views of the surrounding countryside.

These platforms offer an opportunity to savor the gradual unveiling of the expansive vista.

Broadway Village Below:

Gaze down at the picturesque village of Broadway below. The juxtaposition of the quaint cottages against the green landscape creates a timeless scene that is quintessentially Cotswold.

Panoramic Vistas:

Reach the summit and be rewarded with panoramic vistas that stretch as far as the eye can see. The undulating hills, patchwork fields, and meandering lanes form a captivating mosaic beneath an expansive sky.

360-Degree Views:

Engage in a sensory feast as you absorb the 360-degree views from the tower's platform. The Cotswolds unfold in all directions, revealing a landscape that embodies the region's timeless beauty.

Serenity and Tranquility:

Experience a sense of serenity and tranquility at the top of Broadway Tower. The elevation provides a unique perspective, fostering a connection with the natural surroundings and a moment of peaceful reflection.

Changing Seasons and Light:

Appreciate how the scenery transforms with the changing seasons and the play of light. Whether bathed in the warm hues of sunset or adorned with the delicate colors of spring, each visit to Broadway Tower unveils a new chapter in the Cotswold landscape.

Wildlife Watching:

Bring binoculars to indulge in wildlife watching. The elevated position offers a bird's-eye view of the countryside, and you may spot deer, birds, or other wildlife amidst the greenery.

Photographic Opportunities:

Capture the essence of the Cotswolds through your lens. The tower provides a myriad of photographic opportunities, from wide-angle shots of the landscape to close-ups of architectural details.

Descend with Contentment:

Descend from the tower with contentment, knowing that you've captured a piece of the Cotswolds' magic. The memories of the climb and the sweeping vistas will linger as a cherished part of your Cotswold journey.

Climbing Broadway Tower for panoramic vistas is not just a physical ascent; it's a journey through history, architecture, and the sublime beauty of the Cotswolds. Each step toward the summit is a step toward a heightened appreciation of this timeless landscape, leaving an indelible mark on your Cotswold adventure.

BALLOON PHOTOGRAPHY EXCURSION

Embark on a visual odyssey as you soar above the Cotswolds in a hot air balloon, capturing breathtaking aerial perspectives of this enchanting landscape. A balloon photography excursion is not just a journey; it's a canvas of expansive vistas, rolling hills, and charming villages waiting to be immortalized through your lens.

Pre-Flight Excitement:

Begin your balloon photography adventure with a sense of anticipation as you arrive at the launch site. The pre-flight excitement builds as the balloon takes shape against the canvas of the sky.

Balloon Inflation and Boarding:

Witness the mesmerizing process of balloon inflation. The vibrant colors of the balloon material come to life, and the gentle hiss of the gas burners adds an orchestral note to the atmosphere.

Board the basket and feel the ground gradually give way beneath you as the balloon begins its ascent.

Sunrise or Sunset Departure:

Opt for a sunrise or sunset departure to capture the Cotswolds bathed in soft, golden hues. The changing light creates a dynamic and ever-evolving landscape beneath your lens.

Aerial Canvas Unfolding:

As the balloon rises, witness the Cotswolds as a vast aerial canvas unfolding beneath you. Patchwork fields, meandering rivers, and picturesque villages take on a new perspective from this elevated vantage point.

Silent Drift and Photography:

Experience the serene drift of the balloon through the sky. The absence of engine noise creates a tranquil environment conducive to focused photography.

Capture the panoramic views, adjusting your camera settings to capture the nuances of light and shadow that dance across the landscape.

Charming Villages from Above:

Focus your lens on the charming villages that dot the Cotswolds. From the bird's-eye view, the stone cottages, church spires, and winding streets form a captivating mosaic against the green backdrop.

Rolling Hills and Farmland:

Explore the texture of the rolling hills and farmland below. The patterns of crops, hedgerows, and meadows create a visual rhythm that speaks to the agricultural heritage of the region.

Cotswold Stone Architecture:

Zoom in on the details of Cotswold stone architecture. The warm, honey-colored hues of the buildings stand out against the lush surroundings, creating a striking contrast.

Wildlife Spotting from Above:

Keep an eye out for wildlife as you drift above the countryside. Capture moments of birds in flight, grazing deer, or other creatures that add a touch of wildlife magic to your aerial photography.

Balloon Shadows on the Landscape:

Experiment with capturing the shadows cast by the balloon on the landscape below. The interplay of light and shadow adds depth to your photographs and emphasizes the three-dimensional aspect of the scenery.

360-Degree Panoramas:

Rotate around the basket to capture 360-degree panoramas. The ever-changing scenery offers a wealth of photographic opportunities, and the ability to pivot enhances your creative freedom.

Communication with the Pilot:

Maintain communication with the pilot to position the balloon for optimal photography. A skilled pilot will guide the balloon to showcase the most photogenic aspects of the Cotswolds.

Landscapes Transformed by Seasons:

Plan your balloon photography excursion during different seasons to witness how the landscapes transform. Whether adorned in the vibrant colors of autumn or the soft blooms of spring, each season adds its own magic to the visual narrative.

Gentle Descent and Reflection:

As the balloon gently descends, reflect on the visual feast you've captured. Review your photographs and relish the unique perspectives that only a hot air balloon journey can provide.

Post-Flight Celebration:

Conclude your balloon photography excursion with a post-flight celebration. Share your favorite shots with fellow adventurers and the pilot, creating a collective memory of this extraordinary experience.

A balloon photography excursion over the Cotswolds is not just a photo opportunity; it's a symphony of colors, textures, and perspectives that elevates your connection with this timeless landscape. From the tranquility of the silent drift to the thrill of capturing the Cotswolds from above, each moment is a frame in the visual story of your aerial adventure.

SUNSET WATCHING AT CLEEVE HILL

Immerse yourself in the sublime beauty of the Cotswolds as the day gracefully transitions into twilight during a sunset watching experience at Cleeve Hill. Perched atop the highest point in the Cotswolds, this vantage point offers a front-row seat to a celestial spectacle, inviting you to capture the ethereal hues and tranquil landscapes with your lens.

Arrival at Cleeve Hill:

Begin your journey by arriving at Cleeve Hill, the panoramic viewpoint that stands as a gateway to the splendor of the Cotswolds.

Feel the anticipation build as you approach the hill, the vastness of the surrounding landscape unfolding before you.

Choosing a Viewing Spot:

Explore the various vantage points along Cleeve Hill to find the perfect spot for sunset watching. Each location offers a unique perspective, from open meadows to secluded corners with uninterrupted views.

Golden Hour Beginnings:

Witness the magic of the golden hour as the sun begins its descent. The warm, golden hues cast across the landscape create an enchanting ambiance, setting the stage for the unfolding spectacle.

Cotswold Panorama:

Marvel at the expansive Cotswold panorama that stretches before you. Rolling hills, verdant meadows, and charming villages are bathed in the soft glow of the setting sun, creating a scene straight from a storybook.

Twinkling Villages Below:

Observe the villages below as they gradually twinkle to life with the soft glow of streetlights. The Cotswold stone architecture takes on a warm and inviting aura as the day transitions to night.

Hues of Sunset:

Capture the ever-changing hues of the sunset. From fiery oranges and pinks to soothing purples and blues, the sky transforms into a canvas of colors, reflecting the artistic prowess of nature.

Silhouettes of the Landscape:

Frame the silhouettes of the landscape against the backdrop of the setting sun. Trees, hills, and iconic landmarks become dramatic outlines, adding depth and contrast to your photographic compositions.

Cleeve Hill's Unique Features:

Incorporate Cleeve Hill's unique features into your photographs. The undulating terrain, the iconic trig point, and any other distinct elements become integral components of your sunset images.

Cloud Formations:

Embrace the beauty of cloud formations as they catch the last rays of sunlight. Wispy clouds and vibrant hues create dynamic patterns in the sky, adding an extra layer of interest to your sunset photographs.

Tranquil Moments:

Savor tranquil moments as the sun sinks below the horizon. The stillness of Cleeve Hill during sunset provides an opportunity for reflection and connection with the natural beauty surrounding you.

Wildlife Encounters:

Keep an eye out for wildlife that may emerge during the twilight hours. Deer grazing in the meadows or birds returning to their nests become enchanting subjects for your sunset captures.

Long Exposure Techniques:

Experiment with long exposure techniques to capture the changing colors of the sky and create dreamy effects in your photographs. A tripod will be invaluable for these extended exposures.

Reflections on the Horizon:

Capture reflections of the sunset on the horizon. If there are lakes or ponds nearby, they can serve as mirrors, doubling the beauty of the sky and adding a reflective dimension to your images.

Post-Sunset Glow:

Appreciate the post-sunset glow that bathes the landscape in a soft afterglow. This serene phase offers a different mood and color palette, extending the photographic opportunities.

Timelapse Photography:

Consider trying timelapse photography to encapsulate the entire sunset experience in a captivating sequence. This technique allows you to showcase the evolving colors and atmosphere over a condensed timeframe.

Reflecting on the Experience:

Take a moment to reflect on the experience as darkness settles in. The memories captured through your lens become timeless reminders of the natural beauty and tranquility found atop Cleeve Hill.

Sunset watching at Cleeve Hill is not just a visual feast; it's a journey into the heart of the Cotswolds' allure. As the sun bids farewell to the day, your camera becomes a storyteller, preserving the magic of this celestial performance for you to revisit and share for years to come.

PRACTICAL TIPS

TRANSPORTATION GUIDE

Navigating transportation efficiently is essential for a seamless travel experience. Whether exploring the Cotswolds or venturing beyond, consider the following practical tips to enhance your transportation journey:

Car Rental and Exploration:

Opt for car rental to explore the Cotswolds and nearby regions at your own pace.

Choose a vehicle size that suits your travel group and accommodates any luggage requirements.

Public Transportation:

Utilize the comprehensive public transportation network, including buses and trains, to navigate between towns and cities.

Check schedules and plan routes in advance to optimize your travel time.

Cycling in the Countryside:

Embrace the scenic beauty of the Cotswolds by renting bicycles for a leisurely ride through charming villages and picturesque landscapes.

Research cycling routes and ensure your chosen paths align with your skill level.

Walking Tours and Footpaths:

Explore the Cotswolds on foot by embarking on walking tours or following designated footpaths.

Wear comfortable shoes and check weather conditions before setting out on a walking adventure.

Transportation Apps:

Download transportation apps to access real-time schedules, maps, and updates on public transportation options.

Apps like local bus or train schedules can be invaluable for seamless travel planning.

Parking Considerations:

If using a rental car, familiarize yourself with parking options in towns and villages.

Some locations may have designated parking areas or require payment, so plan accordingly.

Travel Off-Peak Hours:

Consider traveling during off-peak hours to avoid congestion and make the most of your time.

Off-peak travel often provides a more relaxed experience, whether on the road or using public transportation.

Advance Ticket Booking:

Save time and potentially money by booking transportation tickets in advance.

This is particularly relevant for train journeys and popular attractions with specific entry times.

Local Shuttle Services:

Inquire about local shuttle services that might offer convenient transportation within specific regions.

Shuttles can be a practical option for short distances or connecting to attractions.

Weather Preparedness:

Stay informed about the weather forecast, especially during the colder seasons or when engaging in outdoor activities.

Plan for potential delays or changes in transportation schedules due to adverse weather conditions.

Navigation Tools:

Use navigation tools such as GPS devices or smartphone apps to assist with directions.

Offline maps can be handy, especially in areas with limited network coverage.

Language Considerations:

Familiarize yourself with essential transportation-related phrases if traveling to regions where English may not be the primary language.

This can aid communication with locals and transportation staff.

Accessibility Information:

If you have specific mobility requirements, check the accessibility features of transportation options, accommodations, and attractions in advance.

Confirm that your chosen modes of transportation can accommodate any special needs.

Emergency Contacts and Local Services:

Keep a list of emergency contacts and local services, including transportation providers, readily available.

Be aware of nearby service stations, repair facilities, and contact information for rental car agencies.

By incorporating these practical transportation tips into your travel plans, you can enhance the overall efficiency and enjoyment of your journey, whether you're exploring the charming Cotswolds or embarking on adventures beyond.

ACCOMMODATION RECOMMENDATIONS

Choosing the right accommodation is a crucial aspect of a successful travel experience. In the Cotswolds, renowned for its picturesque landscapes and charming villages, consider the following accommodation recommendations to make the most of your stay:

Cotswold Cottages:

- Immerse yourself in the quintessential Cotswold experience by staying in a traditional stone cottage.
- Enjoy the charm of exposed beams, thatched roofs, and cozy interiors for an authentic village atmosphere.

Boutique Inns and Bed & Breakfasts:

- Opt for boutique inns or bed & breakfasts nestled within Cotswold villages for personalized service and local charm.

- These accommodations often offer unique, individually styled rooms and a warm, welcoming ambiance.

Historic Manor Houses:

- Experience luxury and history by staying in a historic manor house or country estate.
- Many manor houses in the Cotswolds have been transformed into elegant hotels, providing a blend of opulence and period charm.

Quaint Village Hotels:

- Choose hotels situated in the heart of quaint Cotswold villages for a central and convenient location.
- Enjoy proximity to local attractions, shops, and dining options within charming village settings.

Farm Stays:

- Embrace the rural character of the Cotswolds by opting for a farm stay.
- Experience life on a working farm, enjoy fresh local produce, and revel in the tranquility of the countryside.

Luxury Spa Retreats:

- Indulge in a luxury spa retreat nestled in the Cotswold countryside for a rejuvenating experience.
- Unwind with spa treatments, wellness activities, and luxurious accommodations surrounded by natural beauty.

Quirky and Unique Accommodations:

- Explore the Cotswolds in style by staying in quirky and unique accommodations, such as converted barns, windmills, or even treehouses.
- These distinctive lodgings offer a memorable and unconventional stay.

Countryside Camping and Glamping:

- Connect with nature by camping or glamping in the tranquil Cotswold countryside.
- Campsites and glamping sites often provide stunning views and a chance to experience the beauty of the outdoors.

Family-Friendly Guesthouses:

- Consider family-friendly guesthouses that cater to the needs of travelers with children.
- Look for accommodations with spacious rooms, family activities, and convenient amenities.

Pet-Friendly Options:

- If traveling with pets, choose pet-friendly accommodations that welcome furry companions.
- Many hotels, cottages, and inns in the Cotswolds offer pet-friendly rooms and facilities.

Accessibility-Focused Accommodations:

- Select accommodations with accessibility features if you have specific mobility requirements.
- Check for ramps, elevators, widened doorways, and other amenities that ensure a comfortable stay.

Scenic Riverside Retreats:

- Experience tranquility by booking accommodations situated along scenic riversides.
- Enjoy the soothing sounds of flowing water and picturesque views for a serene and relaxing stay.

Wellness-Focused Accommodations:

- Choose wellness-focused accommodations that offer yoga sessions, spa facilities, and healthy dining options.
- Enhance your well-being while enjoying the natural beauty of the Cotswolds.

Pre-Booking Considerations:

- Book accommodations in advance, especially during peak seasons, to secure your preferred choices.
- Read reviews and consider recommendations to ensure a positive and enjoyable stay.

By considering these accommodation recommendations, you can tailor your lodging experience to match your preferences and enhance your overall enjoyment of the Cotswolds' unique charm and beauty. Whether you seek rustic charm, luxury, or a blend of both, the Cotswolds offers a diverse range of accommodations to suit every traveler's taste.

LOCAL ETIQUETTE AND CUSTOMS

Immerse yourself in the rich cultural tapestry of the Cotswolds by understanding and respecting local etiquette and customs. These practices contribute to a positive and respectful travel experience:

Greeting Locals:

- Extend a polite greeting when meeting locals. A simple "hello" or "good morning" is often appreciated.

- Handshakes are a common form of greeting, especially in more formal situations.

Respecting Personal Space:

- Be mindful of personal space. While the English are generally polite, maintaining a comfortable distance is customary.
- Physical contact is reserved for closer relationships, and a friendly nod or smile is often sufficient in casual encounters.

Dining Etiquette:

- Wait to be seated in restaurants unless there's a sign indicating otherwise.
- Use utensils appropriately, with the fork in the left hand and the knife in the right while cutting food.
- Indicate you've finished eating by placing your utensils parallel across your plate.

Punctuality:

- Being punctual is a sign of respect. Arrive on time for appointments, meetings, or scheduled activities.
- If you're running late, inform the relevant parties as a courtesy.

Queuing (Standing in Line):

- Queuing is a deeply ingrained cultural practice. Wait your turn in lines, whether at public transport stops, attractions, or other public places.
- Cutting in line is generally considered impolite.

Using "Please" and "Thank You":

- Politeness is highly valued. Use "please" when making requests and "thank you" to express gratitude.
- Expressing appreciation, even for small gestures, is seen as good manners.

Social Drinking Customs:

- If invited for a drink, it's customary to reciprocate the offer or express gratitude.
- "Cheers" is a common toast, and it's customary to maintain eye contact during the toast.

Public Behavior:

- Maintain a respectful demeanor in public spaces. Keep noise levels down and be aware of the impact of your actions on others.
- Avoid loud conversations on public transportation and in quiet areas.

Tipping Practices:

- Tipping is customary in restaurants and for certain services. A standard practice is to leave around 10-15% of the bill.
- Check if a service charge is included in the bill, as additional tipping may not be necessary in such cases.

Gift-Giving Etiquette:

- When presenting a gift, it's polite to open it in front of the giver.
- Small gestures of appreciation, such as bringing a gift when invited to someone's home, are well-received.

Adhering to Local Rules:

- Respect local rules and regulations, whether they pertain to traffic, wildlife conservation, or heritage sites.
- Familiarize yourself with any specific guidelines at tourist attractions.

Cultural Sensitivity:

- Be culturally sensitive, especially when visiting religious sites or participating in local traditions.
- Dress modestly when required, and ask for guidance if unsure about cultural practices.

Environmental Responsibility:

- Practice environmental responsibility by disposing of waste responsibly and adhering to recycling guidelines.
- Respect natural landscapes and wildlife habitats during your explorations.

Engaging in Conversation:

- Engage in friendly conversations with locals. Topics such as the weather, local attractions, and cultural experiences are safe and often appreciated.
- Respectful curiosity about the local culture is generally well-received.

By embracing and embodying local etiquette and customs, you not only demonstrate respect for the Cotswolds' cultural heritage but also enhance your travel experience by fostering positive interactions with the welcoming communities you encounter.

TRAVEL ITINERARY SUGGESTIONS

SOLO TRAVELER

Day 1: Arrival in Cotswolds

Morning: Arrive in the Cotswolds

- Start your solo adventure with a smooth arrival in the charming Cotswolds. Check into your cozy accommodation, whether it's a historic inn or a quaint bed and breakfast.

Afternoon: Explore the Local Village

- Begin your journey by strolling through the cobbled streets of a nearby village. Discover hidden gems, browse local shops, and savor a traditional pub lunch.

Evening: Sunset at Broadway Tower

- Head to Broadway Tower for panoramic sunset views. Capture the picturesque landscapes and embrace the tranquility of the countryside.

Day 2: Nature and Adventure

Morning: Hike the Cotswold Way

- Challenge yourself with a solo hike along the scenic Cotswold Way. Enjoy the fresh air and breathtaking views as you traverse through rolling hills and picturesque landscapes.

Afternoon: Picnic in Hidcote Manor Gardens

- Indulge in a peaceful afternoon picnic amid the stunning surroundings of Hidcote Manor Gardens. Relax, read a book, or simply soak in the beauty of well-manicured landscapes.

Evening: Sunset Kayaking on the River Thames

- Embark on a solo kayaking adventure on the River Thames. Paddle along the gentle currents as the sun sets, casting a warm glow on the tranquil waters.

Day 3: Cultural Immersion

Morning: Visit Shakespeare's Birthplace in Stratford-upon-Avon

- Immerse yourself in literary history by visiting Shakespeare's Birthplace. Explore the exhibits and gain insights into the life of the world-renowned playwright.

Afternoon: Explore Gloucester Cathedral

- Wander through the awe-inspiring Gloucester Cathedral. Marvel at the stunning architecture, intricate stained glass, and the rich history encapsulated within the cathedral walls.

Evening: Attend a Local Arts Festival

- Immerse yourself in the local arts scene by attending a cultural festival or performance. Engage with the vibrant artistic community of the Cotswolds.

Day 4: Culinary Delights

Morning: Traditional Afternoon Tea

- Indulge in a leisurely morning with a traditional Cotswold afternoon tea. Enjoy delicate pastries, sandwiches, and the finest local teas in a charming tearoom.

Afternoon: Taste Local Ciders and Cheeses

- Visit a local cider farm and cheese producer for a delightful tasting experience. Savor the flavors of the region's best ciders and cheeses.

Evening: Cotswold Food Tour

- Join a guided food tour to discover the culinary treasures of the Cotswolds. Sample local specialties and immerse yourself in the region's gastronomic delights.

Day 5: Outdoor Adventures

Morning: Hot Air Balloon Ride

- Soar above the countryside on a hot air balloon ride. Experience the breathtaking beauty of the Cotswolds from a unique perspective.

Afternoon: Horseback Riding

- Enjoy a solo horseback riding excursion through the scenic Cotswold Hills. Explore picturesque trails and connect with nature on this equestrian adventure.

Evening: Kayaking on the River Thames

- Conclude your day with a solo kayaking expedition on the tranquil waters of the River Thames. Paddle along as the sun sets, casting a golden hue on the riverbanks.

Day 6: History and Landmarks

Morning: Tour Sudeley Castle

- Explore the historic Sudeley Castle, delving into its rich history and grandeur. Wander through the gardens and discover the tales embedded within the castle walls.

Afternoon: Discover the Rollright Stones

- Visit the mysterious Rollright Stones, an ancient stone circle shrouded in folklore. Reflect on the spiritual and historical significance of this enigmatic site.

Evening: Explore the Ruins of Hailes Abbey

- End the day with a visit to the hauntingly beautiful ruins of Hailes Abbey. Absorb the serene atmosphere and contemplate the centuries of history within these remnants.

Day 7: Shopping and Markets

Morning: Browse the Cotswold Farmers' Markets

- Immerse yourself in the vibrant atmosphere of the Cotswold Farmers' Markets. Discover locally produced goods, artisan crafts, and fresh produce.

Afternoon: Antique Hunting in Stow-on-the-Wold

- Explore the antique shops of Stow-on-the-Wold. Uncover hidden treasures, unique artifacts, and timeless pieces as you wander through this historic market town.

Evening: Shop for Local Crafts in Chipping Campden

- Conclude your shopping spree in Chipping Campden, known for its local crafts. Support local artisans and find souvenirs that capture the essence of the Cotswolds.

Day 8: Festivals and Events

Morning: Cheltenham Literature Festival

- Dive into the world of literature at the Cheltenham Literature Festival. Attend author talks, book signings, and literary discussions in this renowned literary event.

Afternoon: Cotswold Lavender Harvest

- Join the Cotswold Lavender Harvest and immerse yourself in a sea of fragrant blooms. Wander through lavender fields and capture the beauty of this seasonal spectacle.

Evening: Painswick Rococo Garden Snowdrop Week

- Celebrate the enchanting Snowdrop Week at Painswick Rococo Garden. Explore the illuminated gardens adorned with delicate snowdrops in a magical evening setting.

Day 9: Relaxation and Wellness

Morning: Spa Day in a Cotswold Retreat

- Treat yourself to a rejuvenating spa day in one of the Cotswold retreats. Unwind with massages, saunas, and therapeutic treatments.

Afternoon: Yoga Retreat in the Countryside

- Join a solo yoga retreat amidst the tranquil Cotswold countryside. Reconnect with your inner self and find serenity in the peaceful surroundings.

Evening: Thermal Bath Experience in Bath

- Conclude your wellness day with a thermal bath experience in the historic city of Bath. Soak in the therapeutic waters and reflect on your journey through the Cotswolds.

Day 10: Practical Tips and Reflections

Morning: Transportation Guide

- Start your day with a comprehensive review of transportation options for your onward journey. Plan your route and transportation method for a smooth departure.

Afternoon: Local Etiquette and Customs

- Gain insights into local etiquette and customs of the Cotswolds. Appreciate the cultural nuances and traditions that define the region.

Evening: Conclusion and Reflections

- Reflect on your solo adventure in the Cotswolds. Jot down your favorite moments, lessons learned, and the personal growth achieved during this enriching journey.

This solo travel itinerary through the Cotswolds combines cultural exploration, outdoor adventures, culinary delights, and moments of tranquility, offering a diverse and enriching experience for the solo traveler.

ROMANTIC GETAWAYS

Day 1: Romantic Arrival in the Cotswolds

Morning: Arrive at a Charming Inn

- Begin your romantic getaway by checking into a charming inn or boutique bed and breakfast. Choose accommodation with cozy rooms and a touch of historic charm.

Afternoon: Explore a Quaint Village

- Take a leisurely stroll through a quaint Cotswold village. Discover charming cottages, browse local shops hand in hand, and enjoy a romantic lunch at a traditional pub.

Evening: Candlelit Dinner

- Indulge in a candlelit dinner at a romantic restaurant. Savor local delicacies and fine wines in an intimate setting to kick off your romantic escape.

Day 2: Nature and Tranquility

Morning: Private Hot Air Balloon Ride

- Begin your day with a private hot air balloon ride over the serene Cotswold countryside. Drift together above picturesque landscapes for a breathtaking experience.

Afternoon: Picnic in Secluded Gardens

- Enjoy a romantic picnic in the secluded gardens of Hidcote Manor. Spread a blanket, savor gourmet treats, and bask in the beauty of well-manicured landscapes.

Evening: Sunset Kayaking on the Thames

- Embrace the romance of a sunset kayaking adventure on the River Thames. Paddle gently as the sun sets, casting a warm glow on the tranquil waters.

Day 3: Cultural Experiences for Two

Morning: Private Tour of Shakespeare's Birthplace

- Embark on a private tour of Shakespeare's Birthplace in Stratford-upon-Avon. Immerse yourselves in the Bard's world with a knowledgeable guide.

Afternoon: Romantic Stroll in Gloucester Cathedral

- Take a romantic stroll through Gloucester Cathedral. Admire the awe-inspiring architecture and share quiet moments in this atmospheric setting.

Evening: Private Cultural Performance

- Enjoy a private cultural performance or concert in a historic venue. Immerse yourselves in the arts for an intimate and memorable evening.

Day 4: Culinary Delights

Morning: Gourmet Breakfast in Bed

- Begin your day with a gourmet breakfast served in the comfort of your accommodation. Enjoy a lazy morning together.

Afternoon: Cooking Class for Two

- Take a private cooking class to create a romantic meal together. Learn from a local chef and savor your culinary creations.

Evening: Fine Dining Experience

- Conclude your culinary day with a fine dining experience. Choose a restaurant known for its exquisite cuisine and intimate ambiance.

Day 5: Outdoor Adventures for Couples

Morning: Horseback Riding in the Hills

- Embark on a romantic horseback riding excursion through the scenic Cotswold Hills. Explore picturesque trails and create lasting memories together.

Afternoon: Private Guided Cycling Tour

- Join a private guided cycling tour through quaint villages. Cycle side by side, exploring the countryside at your own pace.

Evening: Sunset Balloon Photography

- Capture the magic of the sunset with a private hot air balloon photography excursion. Create timeless memories as you soar above the landscape.

Day 6: Historic Landmarks and Hidden Gems

Morning: Private Tour of Sudeley Castle

- Enjoy a private tour of Sudeley Castle. Delve into the rich history and explore the gardens hand in hand.

Afternoon: Discover Hidden Gardens

- Explore hidden gardens off the beaten path. Stroll through secret corners and revel in the tranquility of lesser-known landscapes.

Evening: Stargazing in a Romantic Setting

- Conclude your day with stargazing in a romantic setting. Whether it's a quiet garden or a private terrace, appreciate the night sky together.

Day 7: Shopping and Markets

Morning: Cotswold Farmers' Markets

- Experience the vibrant atmosphere of Cotswold Farmers' Markets. Sample local delights, pick up handmade crafts, and enjoy the market ambiance.

Afternoon: Antique Hunting and Local Crafts

- Go antique hunting in Stow-on-the-Wold and explore local crafts in Chipping Campden. Find unique treasures and keepsakes together.

Evening: Romantic Dinner in a Vineyard

- Indulge in a romantic dinner in a Cotswold vineyard. Savor exquisite wines and culinary delights in a picturesque setting.

Day 8: Festivals and Events

Morning: Cheltenham Literature Festival

- Attend a cultural event together, such as the Cheltenham Literature Festival. Engage with authors and enjoy literary discussions.

Afternoon: Lavender Harvest Experience

- Join the Cotswold Lavender Harvest for a sensory experience. Wander through lavender fields hand in hand, surrounded by fragrant blooms.

Evening: Private Garden Celebration

- Conclude the day with a private celebration in a garden adorned with fairy lights. Toast to your romantic getaway and enjoy a moment of pure intimacy.

Day 9: Relaxation and Wellness

Morning: Couples Spa Day

- Treat yourselves to a couples spa day in a tranquil Cotswold retreat. Rejuvenate with massages, hot tubs, and relaxation.

Afternoon: Yoga Retreat for Two

- Join a private yoga retreat in the countryside. Connect with each other and nature in a serene and peaceful setting.

Evening: Thermal Bath Experience

- Conclude your wellness day with a thermal bath experience in Bath. Unwind together and reflect on your journey.

Day 10: Romantic Farewell

Morning: Breakfast in a Scenic Spot

- Enjoy a romantic breakfast in a scenic spot, perhaps a garden or overlooking rolling hills. Savor your last moments in the Cotswolds together.

Afternoon: Final Moments in a Charming Village

- Spend your final afternoon in a charming Cotswold village. Explore a few more hidden corners, have a leisurely lunch, and make memories to cherish.

Evening: Sunset Watching at Cleeve Hill

- Conclude your romantic getaway with a spectacular sunset watching experience at Cleeve Hill. Reflect on your journey as you enjoy the breathtaking views together.

This romantic getaway itinerary through the Cotswolds is designed to create unforgettable moments for couples, blending nature, culture, culinary delights, and intimate experiences in the heart of one of England's most picturesque regions.

FAMILY FRIENDLY

Day 1: Welcoming Arrival in the Cotswolds

Morning: Arrive at Family-Friendly Accommodation

- Begin your family adventure by checking into a comfortable and family-friendly accommodation. Opt for a cozy cottage or family suite in a charming inn.

Afternoon: Explore the Local Village

- Take a leisurely stroll through a nearby Cotswold village. Discover family-friendly attractions, such as quaint shops, parks, and perhaps a traditional sweet shop.

Evening: Family Dinner at a Local Pub

- Enjoy a relaxed family dinner at a local pub known for its kid-friendly atmosphere. Savor traditional pub fare and unwind after your journey.

Day 2: Nature and Outdoor Fun

Morning: Cotswold Wildlife Safari

- Kick off the day with a family-friendly wildlife safari in the Cotswolds. Explore nature reserves or wildlife parks for an interactive experience.

Afternoon: Picnic in a Scenic Spot

- Pack a picnic and head to a scenic spot, perhaps a local park or nature reserve. Let the kids run and play while enjoying a family meal amid nature.

Evening: Outdoor Movie Night

- Set up a cozy outdoor movie night in the garden of your accommodation. Bring blankets, popcorn, and enjoy a family-friendly film under the stars.

Day 3: Cultural Discoveries for All Ages

Morning: Visit a Family-Friendly Museum

- Explore a family-friendly museum or interactive exhibit in the Cotswolds. Engage in educational and entertaining activities suitable for all ages.

Afternoon: Storybook Village Exploration

- Discover a storybook village where the streets seem straight out of a fairy tale. Let the kids imagine and play in this enchanting setting.

Evening: Family-Friendly Pub Quiz

- Head to a family-friendly pub for an evening filled with laughter and learning. Participate in a pub quiz suitable for all ages.

Day 4: Outdoor Adventures for the Whole Family

Morning: Family-Friendly Hike

- Embark on a family-friendly hike along well-marked trails. Choose a route with scenic views and manageable distances for everyone.

Afternoon: Family Picnic at a Playground

- Have a family picnic at a local playground. Combine outdoor play with a delicious lunch for a delightful afternoon.

Evening: Evening Stroll in a Riverside Park

- Wind down with an evening stroll in a riverside park. Enjoy the tranquil surroundings and maybe spot some wildlife.

Day 5: Creative Workshops and Culinary Delights

Morning: Family Craft Workshop

- Engage in a family craft workshop where everyone can unleash their creativity. Create mementos to remember your Cotswold adventure.

Afternoon: Local Bakery Visit

- Visit a local bakery for a hands-on baking experience. Let the kids decorate their own treats and enjoy the delicious results.

Evening: Family Dinner with Local Flavors

- Enjoy a family dinner at a restaurant known for its local flavors. Sample traditional dishes with a family-friendly twist.

Day 6: Historic Exploration and Hidden Gems

Morning: Family-Friendly Castle Tour

- Explore a family-friendly castle where the kids can immerse themselves in history. Look for interactive exhibits and guided tours suitable for all ages.

Afternoon: Discover Hidden Gardens

- Stumble upon hidden gardens off the beaten path. Let the kids roam freely and explore these secret corners.

Evening: Stargazing Family Night

- Conclude the day with a stargazing family night. Head to a location away from city lights for a magical evening under the stars.

Day 7: Shopping and Markets for All Ages

Morning: Family Visit to Cotswold Farmers' Markets

- Experience the lively atmosphere of Cotswold Farmers' Markets. Let the kids interact with local vendors and discover fresh produce and handmade crafts.

Afternoon: Family-Friendly Shopping Spree

- Enjoy a family-friendly shopping spree in a market town. Look for toy shops, sweet stores, and places where everyone can find something special.

Evening: Family Movie Night

- Have a cozy family movie night in your accommodation. Bring out the snacks and enjoy a film together.

Day 8: Festivals and Fun for Everyone

Morning: Family-Friendly Festival Visit

- Check out any family-friendly festivals or events happening in the area. Engage in festivities suitable for all ages.

Afternoon: Outdoor Family Games

- Set up a series of outdoor family games in a local park. Enjoy quality time together with activities like sack races, frisbee, or a simple game of catch.

Evening: Family Dinner with Entertainment

- Choose a family-friendly restaurant with entertainment. Whether it's live music, storytelling, or themed nights, make it a memorable family dinner.

Day 9: Relaxation and Wellness for All

Morning: Family Yoga Session

- Begin the day with a family-friendly yoga session. Find a serene spot and engage in gentle exercises suitable for all ages.

Afternoon: Leisurely Afternoon at a Family Spa

- Treat the family to a leisurely afternoon at a family spa. Enjoy pools, play areas, and relaxation for everyone.

Evening: Family Board Game Night

- Conclude your day with a family board game night. Bring out classic board games and enjoy some friendly competition.

Day 10: Farewell with Memories

Morning: Family Breakfast at a Local Café

- Enjoy a family breakfast at a local café. Reflect on the memories created during your Cotswolds adventure.

Afternoon: Final Exploration of a Charming Village

- Spend your final afternoon exploring the streets of a charming Cotswold village. Pick up last-minute souvenirs and cherish your final moments in the picturesque surroundings.

Evening: Sunset Watching at a Family-Friendly Spot

- Find a family-friendly spot to watch the sunset together. Reflect on your family adventure in the Cotswolds and capture the beauty of the moment.

This family-friendly itinerary in the Cotswolds is crafted to cater to all ages, combining outdoor adventures, cultural discoveries, creative workshops, and moments of relaxation for a memorable family getaway.

ADVENTURE ENTHUSIAST

Day 1: Arrival and Orientation

Morning: Arrive in a Picturesque Town

- Kick off your adventure in the Cotswolds by arriving in a charming town surrounded by rolling hills. Check into accommodation that offers a blend of comfort and rustic charm.

Afternoon: Adventure Briefing

- Spend the afternoon getting an adventure briefing from local guides. Familiarize yourself with the upcoming activities and safety measures for an exhilarating experience.

Evening: Welcome Dinner in a Cozy Pub

- Enjoy a welcome dinner at a cozy pub, immersing yourself in the warm ambiance of Cotswold hospitality. Relax and prepare for the thrilling days ahead.

Day 2: Mountain Biking and Nature Exploration

Morning: Mountain Biking in Cranham Woods

- Begin your adventure with an adrenaline-pumping mountain biking expedition in Cranham Woods. Navigate through trails surrounded by lush greenery and challenging terrains.

Afternoon: Forest Picnic and Relaxation

- Take a break with a picnic in the heart of the woods. Recharge amidst nature, surrounded by the sounds of the forest, before gearing up for the next adventure.

Evening: Campfire Gathering

- Conclude the day with a campfire gathering. Share stories with fellow adventurers and relish the camaraderie of like-minded thrill-seekers.

Day 3: Kayaking and Riverside Exploration

Morning: Kayaking on the River Thames

- Embark on an exciting kayaking expedition on the scenic River Thames. Paddle through gentle currents, explore hidden coves, and embrace the adventure on the water.

Afternoon: Riverside Picnic and Relaxation

- Enjoy a riverside picnic with a selection of local treats. Take in the serene surroundings and prepare for the next water-based adventure.

Evening: Cotswold Pub Experience

- Head to a traditional Cotswold pub for a hearty dinner and a chance to swap adventure stories with locals and fellow enthusiasts.

Day 4: Rock Climbing and Cliff Views

Morning: Rock Climbing Excursion

- Gear up for a rock climbing adventure in a designated climbing area. Conquer cliffs, scale heights, and revel in the thrill of reaching new summits.

Afternoon: Cliff-top Lunch

- Enjoy a cliff-top lunch with panoramic views as your reward for the morning's climbing achievements. Take in the breathtaking landscapes surrounding you.

Evening: Sunset Watching at a Scenic Vista

- Unwind with an evening of sunset watching at a scenic vista. Absorb the colors of the sky as the sun sets over the Cotswold hills.

Day 5: Hot Air Balloon Ride and Aerial Views

Morning: Hot Air Balloon Ride

- Soar high above the Cotswold landscapes on a hot air balloon ride. Experience breathtaking aerial views of charming villages and sprawling countryside.

Afternoon: Vineyard Exploration and Wine Tasting

- Explore a Cotswold vineyard post-flight. Indulge in a wine tasting experience, savoring local vintages amidst the picturesque vineyard setting.

Evening: Dinner at a Countryside Inn

- Conclude the day with a hearty dinner at a countryside inn. Enjoy a meal crafted from locally sourced ingredients in a relaxed, rural atmosphere.

Day 6: Horseback Riding and Countryside Trails

Morning: Horseback Riding in the Cotswold Hills

- Embark on a horseback riding adventure through the scenic Cotswold Hills. Explore countryside trails, meadows, and woodlands on horseback.

Afternoon: Picnic in a Secluded Meadow

- Pause for a picnic in a secluded meadow. Experience the tranquility of nature and connect with the serene beauty of the Cotswold countryside.

Evening: Traditional Pub Fare and Live Music

- Head to a traditional pub for a lively evening. Enjoy local pub fare and live music, immersing yourself in the lively atmosphere.

Day 7: Ziplining and Treetop Adventures

Morning: Treetop Ziplining Adventure

- Embark on a thrilling treetop ziplining adventure. Experience the rush as you glide through the canopy, enjoying a unique perspective of the Cotswold landscape.

Afternoon: Forest Canopy Lunch

- Enjoy a lunch suspended in the forest canopy. Savor local delights while surrounded by the natural beauty of the treetops.

Evening: Sunset Hike and Stargazing

- Conclude the day with a sunset hike to a viewpoint. As darkness falls, indulge in some stargazing, appreciating the unpolluted skies of the Cotswolds.

Day 8: Caving Expedition and Underground Exploration

Morning: Caving Expedition

- Delve into an underground caving expedition. Explore hidden caves, tunnels, and formations, experiencing the thrill of underground adventure.

Afternoon: Pub Lunch in a Picturesque Village

- After resurfacing, enjoy a pub lunch in a picturesque Cotswold village. Savor local specialties and unwind in the post-caving glow.

Evening: Fireside Tales and Relaxation

- Gather around a fireside for tales of adventure and relaxation. Share experiences and unwind in the warmth of the firelight.

Day 9: Archery and Historical Pursuits

Morning: Archery Session

- Channel your inner archer with a morning of archery. Test your skills in precision and focus in the beautiful Cotswold countryside.

Afternoon: Visit Historic Landmarks

- Explore historic landmarks, castles, or ancient sites in the Cotswolds. Immerse yourself in the rich history and cultural heritage of the region.

Evening: Farewell Adventure Dinner

- Celebrate the culmination of your adventurous journey with a farewell dinner. Share memories and toast to the experiences that defined your Cotswold adventure.

Day 10: Reflections and Departure

Morning: Adventure Reflections

- Spend the morning reflecting on your thrilling adventures in the Cotswolds. Capture your thoughts, achievements, and the moments that made your journey unforgettable.

Afternoon: Departure

- Bid farewell to the Cotswolds, departing with a sense of accomplishment and a treasure trove of adventure memories. Carry the spirit of the Cotswold thrill with you as you head home.

This Adventure Enthusiast Itinerary in the Cotswolds offers an adrenaline-fueled journey through stunning landscapes, combining outdoor pursuits, unique experiences, and the natural beauty of this enchanting region.

ARTS AND CULTURE EXPLORATION

Day 1: Arrival and Introduction to Cotswolds Arts Scene

Morning: Arrival at a Cultural Hub

- Begin your journey by arriving at a cultural hub in the Cotswolds, known for its artistic atmosphere. Check into accommodation surrounded by galleries and performance spaces.

Afternoon: Explore Local Art Galleries

- Immerse yourself in the local art scene by exploring nearby galleries. Admire contemporary and traditional artworks showcasing the talent of Cotswold artists.

Evening: Welcome Dinner with Cultural Performances

- Enjoy a welcome dinner at a restaurant with live cultural performances. Experience the region's artistic expressions while savoring a delicious meal.

Day 2: Literary Heritage and Creative Workshops

Morning: Jane Austen Trail in Chawton

- Embark on a literary journey with the Jane Austen Trail in Chawton. Visit places associated with the renowned author and explore the settings that inspired her novels.

Afternoon: Writing Retreat in the Cotswold Countryside

- Participate in a writing retreat amidst the picturesque Cotswold countryside. Engage with fellow writers and draw inspiration from the serene surroundings.

Evening: Literary Dinner and Discussion

- Conclude the day with a literary-themed dinner and discussion. Share insights, exchange ideas, and immerse yourself in the world of literature.

Day 3: Historic Landmarks and Cultural Heritage

Morning: Tour Sudeley Castle

- Explore the historical Sudeley Castle, delving into its rich heritage and cultural significance. Discover the art, architecture, and stories that define this landmark.

Afternoon: Discover the Rollright Stones

- Visit the ancient Rollright Stones, a site with historical and cultural importance. Reflect on the mystical aura of these standing stones.

Evening: Cultural Documentary Screening

- Attend a screening of a cultural documentary related to the Cotswolds. Gain insights into the region's history, traditions, and artistic influences.

Day 4: Arts and Crafts Exploration

Morning: Artisan Workshops in Tetbury

- Explore artisan workshops in Tetbury, where local craftspeople create unique and handmade goods. Witness the creative process and perhaps participate in a workshop.

Afternoon: Pottery Class in Chipping Campden

- Engage in a pottery class in the charming town of Chipping Campden. Unleash your creativity while learning the art of pottery.

Evening: Attend a Local Arts Festival

- Immerse yourself in the local arts scene by attending a cultural festival. Experience live performances, art exhibitions, and interact with local artists.

Day 5: Scenic Views and Artistic Inspiration

Morning: Capture Scenic Views at Broadway Tower

- Climb Broadway Tower to capture panoramic vistas. Let the breathtaking scenery inspire your artistic expressions.

Afternoon: Balloon Photography Excursion

- Embark on a hot air balloon photography excursion. Capture artistic aerial views of the Cotswold landscapes.

Evening: Sunset Watching at Cleeve Hill

- Conclude the day by watching the sunset at Cleeve Hill. Absorb the colors of the sky and let the natural beauty inspire your artistic senses.

Day 6: Festivals, Events, and Local Arts

Morning: Attend the Cheltenham Literature Festival

- Participate in the Cheltenham Literature Festival, a hub for literary enthusiasts. Attend author talks, book signings, and engage in discussions.

Afternoon: Cotswold Lavender Harvest Experience

- Join the Cotswold Lavender Harvest for a sensory experience. Wander through lavender fields and capture the essence of this seasonal event.

Evening: Painswick Rococo Garden Snowdrop Week

- Celebrate the enchanting Snowdrop Week at Painswick Rococo Garden. Experience the garden illuminated with delicate snowdrops.

Day 7: Cultural Immersion and Local Performances

Morning: Gloucester Cathedral Art Exhibition

- Explore an art exhibition within the grandeur of Gloucester Cathedral. Admire the juxtaposition of contemporary art in a historic setting.

Afternoon: Cotswold Arts Showcase

- Attend a local arts showcase featuring the works of Cotswold artists. Engage with the creative community and appreciate diverse artistic expressions.

Evening: Cultural Performance in Stratford-upon-Avon

- Attend a cultural performance in Stratford-upon-Avon. Whether it's a play, musical, or dance performance, enjoy the artistic offerings in this iconic town.

Day 8: Culinary Arts and Local Delicacies

Morning: Culinary Workshop with Local Ingredients

- Participate in a culinary workshop using local Cotswold ingredients. Learn the art of creating dishes that reflect the region's flavors.

Afternoon: Wine Tasting in Cotswold Vineyards

- Indulge in a wine tasting experience in Cotswold vineyards. Explore the artistry of winemaking while savoring local vintages.

Evening: Traditional Cotswold Feast

- Conclude the day with a traditional Cotswold feast. Enjoy a culinary journey through local specialties in an artistic setting.

Day 9: Hidden Gems and Local Artistry

Morning: Secret Gardens Off the Beaten Path

- Discover secret gardens off the beaten path. Explore lesser-known horticultural gems that inspire local artists.

Afternoon: Local Artisan Workshops in Tetbury

- Dive deeper into Tetbury's artisan workshops. Engage with local craftspeople, witness their artistic processes, and acquire unique handmade items.

Evening: Cultural Evening in a Historic Venue

- Enjoy a cultural evening in a historic venue. Attend a performance or exhibition that highlights the region's artistic heritage.

Day 10: Reflections on Arts and Culture Exploration

Morning: Cultural Reflections

- Spend the morning reflecting on your arts and culture exploration in the Cotswolds. Capture your thoughts, experiences, and artistic inspirations.

Afternoon: Farewell in a Cultural Setting

- Bid farewell to the Cotswolds in a cultural setting. Whether it's a final visit to an art gallery or a moment of reflection in a historic site, conclude your journey with a sense of cultural fulfillment.

This arts and culture exploration itinerary in the Cotswolds combines literary heritage, visual arts, performing arts, culinary arts, and hidden gems to provide a rich and immersive experience for those seeking creative inspiration.

CULINARY EXPLORATION

Day 1: Arrival and Introduction to Cotswold Gastronomy

Morning: Arrival at a Culinary Hub

- Begin your culinary adventure by arriving at a charming Cotswold town known for its gastronomic delights. Check into accommodation surrounded by local eateries and culinary hotspots.

Afternoon: Traditional Afternoon Tea Experience

- Dive into the local culinary scene with a traditional afternoon tea experience. Savor freshly baked scones, clotted cream, and a variety of teas in a charming tea room.

Evening: Welcome Dinner with Local Flavors

- Enjoy a welcome dinner at a restaurant showcasing local flavors. Indulge in Cotswold specialties and savor regional ingredients prepared by skilled chefs.

Day 2: Market Exploration and Cooking Class

Morning: Cotswold Farmers' Markets

- Immerse yourself in the vibrant atmosphere of Cotswold Farmers' Markets. Explore stalls laden with fresh produce, artisanal cheeses, and local specialties.

Afternoon: Cooking Class with Local Ingredients

- Take a cooking class using fresh Cotswold ingredients. Learn from a local chef and prepare a delightful meal that captures the essence of the region's culinary heritage.

Evening: Dinner at a Gastropub

- Conclude the day with dinner at a Cotswold gastropub. Enjoy a menu that emphasizes local and seasonal ingredients in a cozy, pub-style setting.

Day 3: Cider and Cheese Tasting

Morning: Visit a Local Cidery

- Explore a local cidery and learn about the art of cider-making. Taste a variety of ciders, each with its unique flavor profile, and discover the region's rich cider heritage.

Afternoon: Cheese Tasting Session

- Indulge in a cheese tasting session featuring local Cotswold cheeses. Pair them with artisanal bread, crackers, and condiments for a delightful culinary experience.

Evening: Dinner at a Cheese-themed Restaurant

- Enjoy dinner at a restaurant that celebrates cheese. Delight your taste buds with dishes highlighting the diverse and flavorful cheeses of the Cotswolds.

Day 4: Cotswold Food Tour

Morning: Start the Food Tour

- Embark on a Cotswold food tour, exploring various culinary gems. Visit local producers, bakeries, and markets to sample a wide array of gastronomic delights.

Afternoon: Gourmet Picnic with Local Treats

- Create a gourmet picnic using the treats acquired during the food tour. Find a scenic spot to enjoy a leisurely lunch surrounded by the beauty of the Cotswold countryside.

Evening: Dinner at an Acclaimed Restaurant

- Conclude the day with dinner at an acclaimed Cotswold restaurant. Delve into a menu that showcases the best of local and seasonal ingredients.

Day 5: Traditional Cotswold Feast

Morning: Relaxing Breakfast

- Begin your day with a leisurely breakfast at your accommodation. Enjoy local jams, pastries, and a cup of freshly brewed coffee.

Afternoon: Visit a Local Bakery

- Explore a local bakery and indulge in freshly baked goods. Discover unique pastries and desserts that reflect the culinary creativity of the Cotswolds.

Evening: Traditional Cotswold Feast

- Experience a traditional Cotswold feast at a renowned restaurant. Enjoy a multi-course meal featuring classic dishes prepared with a modern twist.

Day 6: Culinary Workshops and Vineyard Visit

Morning: Artisanal Food Workshop

- Engage in an artisanal food workshop, learning techniques from local producers. Participate in crafting specialties like jams, chutneys, or artisan chocolates.

Afternoon: Wine Tasting in Cotswold Vineyards

- Explore Cotswold vineyards and indulge in wine tasting. Sample a variety of local wines, each reflecting the unique terroir of the region.

Evening: Vineyard Dinner Experience

- Conclude the day with a dinner experience at a vineyard. Enjoy a meal paired with exquisite wines while surrounded by the picturesque vineyard landscape.

Day 7: Culinary Adventures and Gourmet Delights

Morning: Gourmet Breakfast in Bed

- Begin the day with a gourmet breakfast served in the comfort of your accommodation. Savor local delicacies and fresh produce.

Afternoon: Explore Chipping Campden's Culinary Scene

- Spend the afternoon exploring the culinary scene of Chipping Campden. Visit cafes, bakeries, and specialty shops to discover gourmet delights.

Evening: Fine Dining Experience

- Conclude the day with a fine dining experience at a renowned restaurant. Delight in a carefully curated menu showcasing the best of Cotswold cuisine.

Day 8: Culinary Delights and Exquisite Desserts

Morning: Attend a Food Festival

- Attend a local food festival featuring a variety of culinary delights. Engage with local producers and chefs, and sample unique dishes.

Afternoon: Indulge in Sweet Treats

- Indulge your sweet tooth by exploring local patisseries and sweet shops. Discover exquisite desserts and treats crafted with precision and creativity.

Evening: Dessert Tasting Menu

- Enjoy an evening dedicated to desserts with a tasting menu at a specialty dessert restaurant. Explore a variety of flavors and textures in a delightful setting.

Day 9: Seafood Feast and Culinary Reflections

Morning: Coastal-inspired Breakfast

- Enjoy a breakfast inspired by coastal flavors, featuring seafood specialties. Delight in fresh catches and flavors reminiscent of the seaside.

Afternoon: Relaxation and Culinary Reflections

- Spend the afternoon in relaxation, perhaps at a spa or scenic spot. Reflect on your culinary journey through the Cotswolds.

Evening: Seafood Feast at a Seaside-themed Restaurant

- Conclude your culinary adventure with a seafood feast at a seaside-themed restaurant. Indulge in dishes highlighting the finest seafood and coastal influences.

Day 10: Farewell Brunch and Culinary Souvenirs

Morning: Farewell Brunch

- Bid farewell to the Cotswolds with a farewell brunch. Choose a restaurant known for its brunch offerings, and savor your last culinary moments in the region.

Afternoon: Culinary Souvenirs

- Before departing, explore local markets or specialty shops for culinary souvenirs. Take home artisanal products, local delicacies, or a bottle of Cotswold gin to savor the memories of your culinary exploration.

This culinary exploration itinerary in the Cotswolds is designed to immerse you in the region's rich gastronomic heritage, from traditional feasts to contemporary culinary delights. Enjoy a diverse range of experiences that showcase the flavors, creativity, and culinary expertise of the Cotswold countryside.

GRAND TOUR

Day 1: Arrival in the Heart of Cotswolds

Morning: Arrive in a Charming Town

- Begin your grand tour by arriving in a charming Cotswold town. Check into a historic inn or boutique hotel to immerse yourself in the region's ambiance.

Afternoon: Explore the Local Market Square

- Stroll through the local market square, surrounded by traditional honey-colored buildings. Discover quaint shops, cafes, and the vibrant atmosphere of Cotswold life.

Evening: Welcome Dinner in a Historic Pub

- Enjoy a welcome dinner in a historic pub, sampling classic Cotswold dishes. Immerse yourself in the warmth of traditional hospitality and authentic flavors.

Day 2: Charming Villages and Countryside Views

Morning: Discover Bibury's Iconic Arlington Row

- Start the day with a visit to Bibury and explore the iconic Arlington Row cottages. Capture the essence of quintessential Cotswold charm amid picturesque landscapes.

Afternoon: Lunch in Bourton-on-the-Water

- Head to Bourton-on-the-Water for a leisurely lunch by the river. Explore the charming village and its delightful bridges, earning its nickname, the "Venice of the Cotswolds."

Evening: Sunset at Cleeve Hill

- Conclude the day by witnessing a breathtaking sunset at Cleeve Hill. Enjoy panoramic vistas of the countryside as the day turns to dusk.

Day 3: Cultural Heritage and Historic Landmarks

Morning: Visit Shakespeare's Birthplace in Stratford-upon-Avon

- Travel to Stratford-upon-Avon to visit Shakespeare's birthplace. Immerse yourself in the Bard's world and explore the historic market town.

Afternoon: Explore Gloucester Cathedral

- Explore the grandeur of Gloucester Cathedral, known for its stunning architecture and rich history. Discover the beauty of its stained glass windows and medieval cloisters.

Evening: Attend a Local Arts Festival

- Immerse yourself in the local arts scene by attending a cultural festival or event. Experience live performances, art exhibitions, and the vibrant creativity of the Cotswolds.

Day 4: Nature and Outdoor Adventures

Morning: Hike the Cotswold Way

- Begin the day with a refreshing hike along the Cotswold Way. Explore scenic trails, charming woodlands, and enjoy the serenity of the countryside.

Afternoon: Picnic in Hidcote Manor Gardens

- Indulge in a picturesque picnic in the renowned Hidcote Manor Gardens. Revel in the beauty of meticulously designed gardens and tranquil surroundings.

Evening: Hot Air Balloon Ride over the Countryside

- Embark on a thrilling hot air balloon ride, offering panoramic views of the Cotswold countryside. Witness the landscapes from a unique and breathtaking perspective.

Day 5: Culinary Delights and Market Exploration

Morning: Indulge in Traditional Afternoon Tea

- Begin your day with a luxurious traditional afternoon tea experience. Savor delicate sandwiches, pastries, and fine teas in an elegant setting.

Afternoon: Taste Local Ciders and Cheeses

- Explore a local cidery and cheese shop, indulging in a tasting experience. Sample a variety of ciders paired with artisanal Cotswold cheeses.

Evening: Culinary Workshop with Local Ingredients

- Participate in a culinary workshop using fresh Cotswold ingredients. Learn the art of crafting local specialties with expert guidance.

Day 6: Historic Landmarks and Literary Heritage

Morning: Tour Sudeley Castle

- Explore the historic Sudeley Castle, surrounded by stunning gardens and steeped in royal history. Discover its fascinating tales and architectural splendor.

Afternoon: Jane Austen Trail in Chawton

- Travel to Chawton and follow the Jane Austen Trail. Visit the author's former home and immerse yourself in the literary heritage of the Cotswolds.

Evening: Sunset Watching at Broadway Tower

- Conclude the day with a visit to Broadway Tower for panoramic views. Watch the sunset over the expansive landscapes of the Cotswolds.

Day 7: Hidden Gems and Family-Friendly Fun

Morning: Discover Hidden Gardens

- Uncover hidden gardens off the beaten path, where tranquility and beauty converge. Immerse yourself in the serenity of lesser-known horticultural gems.

Afternoon: Family-Friendly Farm Park Adventure

- For a family-friendly experience, visit the Cotswold Farm Park. Enjoy interacting with animals, engaging activities, and a fun-filled afternoon for all.

Evening: Ghost Tours by Candlelight

- Join a ghost tour in a historic setting, exploring haunted tales by candlelight. Experience the eerie side of the Cotswolds' history.

Day 8: Outdoor Adventures and Relaxation

Morning: Kayaking on the River Thames

- Engage in an adventurous morning with kayaking on the River Thames. Explore the scenic waterways and embrace the outdoors.

Afternoon: Spa Day in a Cotswold Retreat

- Indulge in an afternoon spa retreat, offering relaxation and rejuvenation. Unwind with massages, thermal baths, and tranquil surroundings.

Evening: Wine Tasting in Cotswold Vineyards

- Conclude the day with a sophisticated wine tasting experience in Cotswold vineyards. Savor local vintages amid the vineyard's serene ambiance.

Day 9: Scenic Views and Literary Heritage

Morning: Capture Scenic Views at Broadway Tower

- Climb Broadway Tower to capture panoramic vistas. Let the breathtaking scenery inspire your senses and creativity.

Afternoon: Literary Retreat in the Cotswold Countryside

- Spend the afternoon in a literary retreat amid the Cotswold countryside. Reflect on your journey, read, or write surrounded by nature.

Evening: Grand Farewell Dinner

- Conclude your grand tour with a grand farewell dinner at a distinguished restaurant. Enjoy a gourmet feast celebrating the culinary diversity of the Cotswolds.

Day 10: Reflections and Departure

Morning: Cultural Reflections

- Spend the final morning reflecting on your grand tour. Capture your thoughts, experiences, and favorite moments.

Afternoon: Departure

- Bid farewell to the Cotswolds with a heart full of memories. Depart from the charming region, taking with you the essence of its landscapes, culture, and rich history.

This grand tour itinerary in the Cotswolds seamlessly combines cultural immersion, outdoor adventures, culinary delights, and family-friendly activities, offering a comprehensive and unforgettable exploration of this enchanting region.

CONCLUSION AND REFLECTIONS

As your journey through the enchanting Cotswolds comes to a close, take a moment to reflect on the myriad experiences that have woven together to create lasting memories. The Cotswolds, with its idyllic landscapes, charming villages, and rich cultural tapestry, offers a tapestry of moments that beckon reflection and appreciation.

Embracing Natural Beauty:

Reflect on the serene beauty of the Cotswolds' rolling hills, lush meadows, and quaint villages. Each landscape tells a story, inviting you to appreciate the timeless allure of the English countryside.

Cultural Immersion:

Consider the cultural immersion experienced in charming villages and historic landmarks. From the Cotswold stone architecture to the echoes of ancient history, the region's cultural richness has left an indelible mark on your journey.

Connection with Locals:

Recall the warmth of connections forged with locals. Whether sharing stories in a cozy tearoom or receiving a friendly greeting on a village stroll, these moments of connection add depth to your travel narrative.

Culinary Delights:

Revisit the flavors and aromas of Cotswold-inspired cuisine. From traditional afternoon teas to savoring local ciders and cheeses, the culinary delights have not only pleased the palate but also provided a taste of the region's gastronomic heritage.

Outdoor Adventures:

Contemplate the thrill of outdoor adventures, whether floating above the countryside in a hot air balloon, horseback riding through the hills, or kayaking on the River Thames. These activities have allowed you to engage with the landscape in dynamic and memorable ways.

Historic Exploration:

Reflect on the exploration of historic landmarks, from the iconic Sudeley Castle to the ancient Rollright Stones and the evocative ruins of Hailes Abbey. Each site has whispered tales of bygone eras and contributed to your understanding of the region's rich history.

Festivals and Events:

Consider the vibrant energy of festivals and events attended, from the literary charm of the Cheltenham Literature Festival to the picturesque scenes of the Cotswold Lavender Harvest and the magical Snowdrop Week at Painswick Rococo Garden.

Relaxation and Wellness:

Revisit the moments of tranquility experienced during spa days, yoga retreats, and thermal bath indulgences. These wellness activities have not only rejuvenated the body but also provided a respite for introspection.

Practical Insights:

Acknowledge the practical tips that have guided your journey, whether navigating transportation seamlessly or adhering to local etiquette. These insights have enhanced the practical aspects of your travels, allowing for a smoother and more immersive experience.

Personal Growth:

Consider the personal growth and introspection fostered by the Cotswolds' serene ambiance. The moments of solitude, coupled with the beauty of nature, have offered an opportunity for self-reflection and renewal.

Gratitude for the Journey:

Express gratitude for the entire journey, encompassing the highs and the quiet moments of contemplation. Each experience, whether grand or subtle, has played a role in creating a holistic and enriching travel experience.

Carrying Memories Forward:

As you bid farewell to the Cotswolds, carry the memories forward. The landscapes, the laughter, the flavors, and the cultural encounters are not just snapshots in time but threads that weave into the fabric of your travel narrative.

In conclusion, the Cotswolds is more than a destination; it's a journey of discovery, connection, and reflection. As you carry the essence of this picturesque region with you, may the memories of your time in the Cotswolds continue to inspire and enrich your future travels and adventures.

Printed in Great Britain
by Amazon

11c055d1-0b4d-49d7-9011-6430e939bc09R01